IOWA PINTS

A Guide to Iowa Breweries
By J. Wilson
author of the *Diary of a Part-time Monk*

Gentry County
Publishing, LLC

$16.95
ISBN 978-0-692-02735-6

Published by
Gentry County Publishing, LLC
213 West Clay Street
Albany, MO 64402
www.aledger.net

The author and publisher encourage all readers to visit the breweries and sample their beers, but recommend that those who consume alcoholic beverages travel with a nondrinking driver.

Printed in the United States of America

First Edition

Cover design by Christy Groves
Photographs by J. Wilson

Labels and logos used with permission of the breweries.

ISBN 978-0-692-02735-6

It seems odd to dedicate a beer
book to someone with a gluten
intolerance who can't even
drink the stuff, but that's what
I have to do. She's been
indispensable.

To Michelle, with thanks

Contents

The Breweries

Appendices

Foreword

I remember having my first beer back in the early 1980s. It was with friends late one night after work behind the Carrolton Inn. It had been a hot night of work, and I was handed a Coors Banquet. I took that ice-cold beer in one hand and with my other hand pinched my nose as I choked that beer down. Not a very auspicious beginning to what now borders on pure obsession and love for one of mankind's greatest achievements.

During my college summer breaks my buddies and I shot pool in my parents' basement, and each time we played we brought a new beer. The beers we drank passed for variety in Carroll, Iowa. It was a tour of light lager cans from some near relic breweries: High Life, Stroh's, Schlitz, Schaefer's, Schmidt's, Falstaff, Hamm's, Old Style, Old Milwaukee, Grain Belt, Pabst, Olympia, and a few I can't recall. These beers were the remnants and shadow of a once great brewing tradition in America. While my buddies and I were sampling our way through America's brewing past, craft beer pioneers and risk takers where already hard at work changing the future of beer in America forever.

During my junior year at college, I had an opportunity to spend a semester at Trinity College in Carmarthen, Wales. My new Welsh friends took me out to their favorite local pubs and introduced me to beers I had never heard of before. I became a regular at The Dairies Sports and Social Club, where I met Bob the bartender. Whenever Bob was behind the bar he would always have a Newcastle (Newky Brown) waiting for me. Newcastle's tag line, "The One and Only," always reminds me that this "One" was responsible for my beer conversion. For holiday breaks from college in Wales we took trips to Belgium with all its unique beers, Munich with its great brewing tradition, and Guinness at the St. James's Gate Brewery opened my eyes to what beer had to offer. The variety that was and is American light lager no longer held its luster.

After school and a move to Des Moines, things were fairly bleak on the beer front. I looked for beers like the ones I had in Europe. A chance encounter with The Old Depot Brewery in Adel on a bicycle ride would change everything. They served pale ale, brown ale, wheat, and stout—all similar to the beers I had in Wales—but these were made in Iowa. What a revelation! I soon found out about other new and exciting beers from the Midwest at a brewfest in Valley Junction. They had different beers from all over, and I knew one thing—I wanted to try them all! It was at this brewfest that my curiosity turned to obsession and the answer to a frequent question was coined.

"What's your favorite beer?"

My reply has thereafter been, "The one I haven't had yet!"

Now, my vacations have a whole new dimension. I travel to cities with a list of bars in hand and do my best to make it to every one. I visit bottle shops and fill my trunk up with beers to enjoy when I got home to Des Moines. Trips to England and Scotland for research before opening the Royal Mile and to Munich to research our concept for Hessen Haus taught me about brewing traditions and beers that inspired so many American brewers. All my experiences with the beer world were great, but my first trip to the Great American Beer Festival in Denver in 2006 was truly mind-blowing.

We headed to Denver with the idea of opening up a multi-tap American craft beer bar. While we were putting the plan for el Bait Shop together, I met Fritz Maytag, Sam Calagione, Michael Jackson (the beer writer), and countless more brewery representatives. I put together a binder for the GABF that talked about our bars and on the cover was a map of the Midwest I had copied off the Bell's Brewing Company website. The cover photo told the story. All of the states around Iowa were colored in, and Iowa was blank. This pretty much summed up what breweries thought of us. We had a feeling though that craft beer was going to become a very big thing in Iowa. The original idea for el Bait Shop went from 35 tap handles to 105 and over 100 bottles of primarily American craft beer (as of now we have 130 tap handles and 250 in bottles). America's craft beer industry was exploding, and the desire for good beer was growing. By this time, Iowa had a handful of breweries open, but something was missing.

The Iowa Beer Equality Law was passed in Iowa in March of 2010, and with it came big changes. Iowa had long suffered prohibition of alcohol; in fact, Iowa had introduced laws to limit alcohol around a half dozen times. Before the law change, Iowa breweries could not produce, and beer wholesalers could not sell, beer over 6.25% alcohol by volume. It really held brewers and distributors back from selling some of the best and most interesting beers the industry had to offer. Now, several new breweries have started up in Iowa, and some of the nation's best breweries' beers are showing up in bars and on store shelves.

The American brewing industry soon will reach a milestone: the most breweries operating in America in the history of the country. It's taken over thirty years to get to this point from the all-time low in the early 1980s. Right alongside this expansion has been an explosion of new breweries in Iowa. We have over 50 breweries in operation or in planning (top one-third in U.S. breweries per capita). Since the law change, the breweries have been making top-notch, high-quality, and award-winning beers. Today we have two or three beer events a week going on in the state at any given time when we used to have two to three events a year. These days, the state's breweries and beer industry are featured in articles in national publications, websites, television, and radio. This brings me to a certain "Beer Drinker of the Year."

I first heard of J. Wilson from a friend of mine, Eric Sorensen, the head brewer at Rock Bottom Restaurant and Brewery in West Des Moines. Eric told me about a guy and his attempt to drink doppelbock beer through Lent for his only nourishment. Growing up in Carroll and raised Catholic, drinking only beer for 46 days oddly seemed to make sense, and I had to meet him. I met J. Wilson at a reception for him at Rock Bottom after being named 2012 "Beer Drinker of the Year" in Denver.

J. and I have since worked together promoting all things beer. We have hosted J. for book signings at el Bait Shop and the Red Monk. J. also had me on his radio program, and he has helped me promote events like the Little Giant Beer Summit of Iowa beers.

The story of the craft beer movement in Iowa and the people who made it happen is a great story, and the passion J. has for beer is a good pairing. This book provides the perfect guide to these terrific breweries in the great state of Iowa.

Jeff Bruning
Owner of el Bait Shop
Des Moines, Iowa

Patrons enjoy a beer in the tap room of the Des Moines Confluence Brewing Company.

Introduction

Welcome to the wonderful world of Iowa beer! If you're like me, I'm sure that Iowa might not be the first place that comes to mind when the words "good" and "beer" are spoken together. Places like Germany, England, and Belgium are sure to top the list, and these days, American cities like Portland, Denver, and San Diego do their work to not only influence the better beer scene stateside, but also to stimulate brewing and drinking in the Old World.

Iowa is no exception to the craft beer boom. We, too, boast the tasty libations.

Like many Midwestern states, Iowa received its fair share of German immigrants between 1840 and 1890. Living their way of life in which beer was an integral part, and recognizing a ripe market, many of these new Iowans set up "backyard" and "basement" breweries to service the needs of a growing population. In the 1850s and 1860s, several, especially along the Mississippi River, prospered, putting out 10-30 barrels of beer per day (a barrel being 31 gallons). A.J. Peaslee & Co. of Dubuque maxed its production capacity at over 2,000 barrels per year. On the western side of the state, The Sioux City Brewery, operated by J. Franz & Co. peaked at 10,000 barrels per year.

Some of the other early breweries sprinkled across the state included Burghart & Fischer of Council Bluffs, H. Frahm of Davenport, Clinton Brewing Company of Clinton, Star Brewery of Dubuque, New Vienna Brewing Company of New Vienna, A. Potthoff of Des Moines, M. Eigenmann of Muscatine, Henne & Schleifer of Mt. Pleasant,

Bensburg & Cheadle of Ottumwa, F.W. Anschutz of Keokuk, and C. Magnus Eagle Brewery of Cedar Rapids.

By the 1870s and early 1880s, breweries shifted from selling primarily draught products to bottling their wares for other markets, which now included Wisconsin, Minnesota, Nebraska, the Dakotas, Colorado, and New Mexico.

Though German-rooted lager brewing slaked thirsts far and wide in the late 19th century, ale brewers like Western Brewery and Pechstein & Nagel of Keokuk and E.C. Peaslee of Dubuque also existed.

But there were drier elements to the population as well. As early as 1854, eight years after becoming a state, Iowa passed a prohibition law, but it proved unenforceable. In 1858, the law was amended to allow the sale of beer and wine made from fruits and grains, but liquor also still flowed.

Fifty-five percent of Iowa voters approved a constitutional amendment in 1882, causing much of Iowa's brewing industry to shut down. However, the law was later declared unconstitutional by the Iowa Supreme Court, as the wording approved by voters differed from what was passed in the General Assembly. Another prohibition law came in 1883, confining alcohol trafficking to pharmacists, who could sell alcohol for medicinal, culinary, or sacramental purposes.

Bootlegging abounded for the thirsty minority. Eventually, a local option law passed in 1893, allowing counties to decide on their own liquor laws.

Some within the industry dabbled in both brewing and malting, or focused on malting alone, with at least three malting companies emerging in Davenport alone—Davenport Malting Company, East Davenport Malt House, and Independent Malting Company. At the turn of the century, many of the smaller Iowa breweries closed or were bought out as larger breweries began to dominate the market. The Eagle Brewery, renamed Mangus Brewing Company after an 1898 change of ownership, survived the industry hiccups, but shuttered in 1916, when a statewide prohibition went into effect. A few of the largest breweries attempted to manufacture non-alcoholic products at this time, but with limited success.

Four years later, the U.S. Congress passed the 18th Amendment, and the "Noble Experiment" was on its way for the entire country. The law was flouted, and organized crime rose, but clearer minds eventually prevailed. Prohibition was repealed in 1933.

Prior to Prohibition, 138 breweries operated in Iowa. After, only two returned: Sioux City Brewing Company and Dubuque Star Brewing Company (formerly Star Brewery). Sioux City Brewing Company was founded in 1899, and was known for Bavarian Export, Extra Pale Select, Heidel Brau and Western Brew. At the time it closed in 1958, it was Iowa's largest brewery.

The Dubuque brewery reopened, but battled flooding on its Mississippi River-front location, with substantial damage to the facility coming in 1965. Joseph Pickett purchased the brewery in 1971, and immediately began a substantial rehab to the facility, now called Joseph Pickett and Sons, though still producing the Dubuque Star brand,

Peace Tree Brewing Company's Shanron Driesen and Taylor Evans keep fans happy at the Iowa Craft Brew Festival in Des Moines.

along with Vat 7. By the late 1970s, his Pickett's Premium had captured 12 percent of the region's market share, a notable feat. But the brewery changed hands a number of times, starting in 1980, closing and reopening repeatedly. In 1982, it was again renamed Dubuque Star. Despite attempts to keep the brewery operational, it closed for good in 1999.

Dubuque Star's woes were mirrored across the country. Iowa, and the whole of the United States, endured a decidedly bland diet where beer was concerned for several decades. Though Iowa native Fritz Maytag would buy and revive a flagging Anchor Brewing Company in San Francisco, California in 1965, and Jack McCauliffe would found New Albion Brewing Company in Sonoma, California in 1976—both cementing their positions as grandfathers of today's craft beer revolution—Iowa wouldn't see a new brewery launch until 1985.

Long overdue, Millstream was the first brewery to operate in Amana since 1884. A trio of brothers, Carroll F. Zuber, James Roemig, and Dennis Roemig, brought character to an insipid liquid landscape. Joseph Pickett consulted to design both the brewhouse and the first two beers, Millstream Lager and Schild Brau. Millstream changed hands in 2000, with the team of Tom and Teresa Albert and Chris Priebe taking the helm. Priebe, a Dubuque Star alumnus, attended (and still does) to the brewhouse details, and, today, Millstream is Iowa's oldest and most award-winning brewery. Schild Brau Amber Lager alone has 16 medals to its credit, including gold medals from the Great American Beer Festival and World Beer Cup.

Millstream was alone in the craft beer market for many years, followed by Davenport's Front Street Brewery in 1992, Des Moines' Court Avenue Restaurant & Brewing

Company (CABCo) in 1996, and Solon's Stone City Brewing Company in 1996. While Millstream and Stone City, the latter now defunct, alone packaged their beer for grocery store shelves (supported by early craft beer cheerleaders at John's Grocery in Iowa City—still a substantial name in the realm of craft beer retail), Front Street and CABCO introduced the brewpub concept to Iowa, and found a loyal following from flavor-starved beer lovers. Eventually more brewpubs would join the market. But these early Iowa craft brewers were hamstrung by antiquated laws that didn't allow them to brew beers above six percent alcohol by weight, while wineries were welcome to produce wines well above this level, hard liquor was available for purchase, and out-of-state breweries were able to distribute beers into Iowa above the six percent threshold.

With Iowa brewers at a competitive disadvantage, the growth of Iowa's craft beer scene was sluggish compared to other parts of the country. But there was still a pull from an informed group of consumers. Homebrewers were free to brew at will, and were always on the hunt for the next beer epiphany. Tap houses like el Bait Shop, established in Des Moines in 2006, were happy to oblige, offering hundreds of beers from craft brewers all across the country, as well as notable imports. This was well and good, but everyone could see that Iowa brewers themselves were grossly outnumbered and functioning with a legislative handicap. Beer lovers around the state joined forces to champion the cause. After a few false starts, the organized effort, Lift the Limit, convinced the Iowa legislature to raise the cap from 6% alcohol by weight (7.6 % ABV) to 12% ABW (15.2% ABV).

Gov. Chet Culver signed SF 2088 in March of 2010, and Iowa breweries have since brewed more beers with more creativity than ever before. At the time, there were in the neighborhood of 20 breweries in the state. Today, just four years later, Iowa boasts over 50 breweries—and the number continues to rise. Beer tourism is a "thing," and the long overdue change in the Iowa Code has brought increased revenue for the state not only from licensing fees and excise taxes from the growing number of brewers, but also from out-of-state visitors who seek out notable beers at their source.

Want a really good Iowa-made hoppy beer? Visit Toppling Goliath Brewing Company in Decorah. Like to play on the water? Visit West O Beer in West Okoboji after a long day's waterskiing. Heading to a Hawkeye game? Don't miss Backpocket Brewing Company in Coralville. Want some barrel-aged magic? Rock Bottom Restaurant and Brewery in West Des Moines can make your palate jump for joy.

More than pigs, corn and quaint communities, Iowa has a beer scene that offers something for everyone. Iowa brewers make world-class light beer, dark beer, sour beer, and smoked beer. Iowa brewers make Belgian styles, German styles, English styles, Czech styles, American styles, and hybrid styles. We have it all, and much of it is darned good, let me assure you.

A word about what is "good," if I might. I'm an award-winning homebrewer, a Certified BJCP (Beer Judge Certification Program) Beer Judge, Wynkoop Brewing Company's 2012 Beer Drinker of the Year, and I formerly worked for a brewery in North

Carolina. I know a thing or two about beer, but I also know that this business of likes and dislikes is subjective as can be. Everyone's palate is different. I may like a beer that you find utterly offensive; you may not notice the profound flaws I pick up in another beer.

The best way to learn about beer, and to learn what *you* like in a beer, is to taste. Visit Iowa's breweries, beer bars and grocery store beer aisles. *Taste*. See what *you* like. Don't avoid the dark stuff. Taste it all. And when you find what you like, go back for more. The economy is depending on you.

Though I may recommend a "must-try" beer now and again, this book is a guidebook, not a book of reviews. I'm sure you can track down a few of my opinions online, but the point of this book is to help you find good beer in Iowa. It's set up in alphabetical order, and each entry will provide information on the beer and the people at each brewery, as well as where they are located and where you can find their beers. With the help of Iowa's brewers and industry insiders, I've compiled appendices of recommended bars/restaurants and stores where you can count on finding a solid beer lineup. I've tracked down a comprehensive list of homebrew shops for those who may want to give brewing at home a try, and a list of Iowa's homebrew clubs for those who want to consort with and learn from like-minded individuals. Herein, you'll find maps, tips, a glossary of beer terms, and the stories behind some of your favorite beers.

And finally, I've pulled together a list of breweries that are "still fermenting." That is, they are breweries-in-planning. As the beer industry is complicated and expensive, there's no way of knowing when or if each of the breweries on this list will ever see the light of day, but on the day this book was published, these were the breweries that were known to be in the works, whether or not they had a name attached to them. This list will clue you in on the ones to watch for in the near future, but in some cases, the brewhouse some guy's got planned out in his head or on his kitchen table is unknowable. So there's more to come, I can assure you. Stay thirsty! Keep your eyes peeled online for their progress.

Who do I like in the world of Iowa Beer? Doesn't matter. I'm friends with many of Iowa's brewers and brewery owners. I've brewed with them. I've drunk with them. I've shared meals with them. I certainly prefer this Iowa beer over that Iowa beer, but that's not what this book is about. It's about *finding* those Iowa beers, so you can decide for yourself. Now, get out there and go to work!

Peace & Pints!

J. Wilson

Beer 101

Beer books of all shapes, sizes, and focuses typically back up and include a section on beer's history, hitting high points such as beer's ancient Sumerian discovery, brewing monks of the Middle Ages, Prohibition and an account of craft beer's revolution, which began in the 1970s. With the exception of the pertinent walk down memory lane with regard to beer and brewing in Iowa that I discussed in the introduction, I covered all the broad beer history I intend to in the preceding sentence.

However, because "beer newbies" as well as veterans will come to possess this book, it makes sense for me to discuss the ingredients utilized in beer's production, as well as how it is made—another ubiquitous element to beer books. But I'll be brief, because as I also noted in the Introduction, this is foremost a guidebook on the beers of Iowa. It is not a brewing textbook.

Malted barley and hot water are combined during mashing, the first step of brewing beer.

The Brewing Process

Beer is made of four principle ingredients: malted barley, hops, yeast, and water. Whether one is brewing five gallons or fifty barrels, the process is the same. Water is combined with malted barley at a temperature between 140° and 158° Fahrenheit. This process, called mashing, converts the starches in the grain to fermentable sugars. Mashing at a lower temperature will result in a more fermentable wort (pronounced wert), which is the name given to this new sugary liquid (it will be called beer only after fermentation), while mashing at the high end of the spectrum will produce a wort with more complex sugars. A lower mash temperature helps to create a lighter-bodied beer (think Pilsner), while a higher mash temperature produces a beer with a fuller body (think Scotch ale).

Once the mashing process (typically an hour or so) is complete, the wort is transferred to the kettle to boil for roughly an hour. This accomplishes several tasks, including sanitizing the wort, concentrating sugars and isomerizing hops (the process of converting alpha acids to iso-alpha acids—making use of the bitterness potential of the resin glands of the hop flowers—to add bitterness and balance to the beer).

As noted, hops are added during the boil. Broadly speaking, the use of hops takes place at three points during the boil—and the beer style in production dictates when hops are used. Most beers incorporate a "bittering" addition. Here, hops are added at the beginning of the boil. As the name suggests, this addition gives beer its bitter character (or at least offsets the malt-derived sweetness). You guessed it—the style being brewed dictates the degree of balance (for example: a Scotch ale leans toward malty-sweet, while an India pale ale leans toward bitter).

The second hop addition, mid-boil, brings hop flavor into the mix, while the third addition, near the end of the boil, adds aroma to the beer (more on hop flavors and aromas in a moment). There's another time for hops, as well. Perhaps you've heard of "dry-hopping"? This hop addition adds yet another big boost of hop-derived aromatics to the beer, and comes after primary fermentation is finished.

Once the boil is complete, the beer is cooled and transferred to a fermenter. Homebrewers will ferment in five-gallon plastic buckets or glass carboys, while professional brewers make use of stainless steel tanks. No matter. Yeast is "pitched" into the vessel to consume the sugars produced during mashing. Depending on the beer style (again) the beer will ferment at anywhere from 45° to 72° Fahrenheit. There are two byproducts of fermentation: carbon dioxide (CO_2) and alcohol. The CO_2 is allowed to escape through an airlock or a blow-off tube, and, once the yeast has metabolized all the sugars, the brewer has a vat of flat beer.

At this point, commercial brewers will often, but not always, filter the beer to improve clarity (and appearance, for the Clear Beer Police). Homebrewers seldom filter their beer.

The next step is conditioning, which is beerspeak for carbonating the beer. This can be done naturally in the bottle or cask by adding a little extra sugar before sealing it off. The yeast consumes this sugar, but with nowhere to go, the CO_2 is dissolved into the solution. Beer can also be force-carbonated by adding CO_2 to a sealed tank. The latter technique is common in commercial brewing, though homebrewers and professional brewers alike employ both techniques. Once carbonated, commercial brewers package the beer (in kegs and/or bottles), and send it out into the market for thirsty beer lovers to track down and consume.

Spent grain from beer production will be picked up by a local farmer to feed to livestock.

The Ingredients

Water

Water accounts for eighty-five to ninety percent of beer, so as uninteresting as water sounds when compared to flashier ingredients like hops, coconuts or bull testicles, it really needs to be our first point of discussion. For a speedy illustration on just how important water is in the flavor profile, take a few minutes to brew two pots of coffee, one using bottled water and another using water scooped straight from an Iowa farm pond. Tell me the bottled water version doesn't taste better. This being the case, quality water is clearly an important aspect to beer quality.

If it's potable, it's usable in brewing, but it still may require a touch of treatment for proper use. It must be boiled, because even tap water carries low concentrations of bacteria. If it is chlorinated, as most tap water is, this must be removed to produce a quality beer. Boiling sheds chlorine gas, but chloramines must be charcoal-filtered.

In order to brew specific styles, it is important to understand water's mineral profile. In the many noted brewing centers of the world, mineral content helped to determine what beers were successful and where. The waters of London, Dublin and Munich, for example, carry a high bicarbonate content and are ideal for acidifying the dark and roasted malts used in stouts, porters and bocks that became popular in these areas. Burton-on-Trent naturally evolved into a suitable location for brewing hoppy bitters and pale ales, as the water in this area is high in sulfate and magnesium, which adds a dryness that accents hop character.

Starting with a neutral water profile, and keeping in mind alkalinity, pH, and water hardness, a brewer can "build" a water profile to suit his purposes in emulating this or that world beer style. This is all very "science-y," and perfect content for a much deeper book on brewing itself. There are many great resources out there, so start digging.

It takes both heavy lifting and button pushing to brew a batch of beer.

Malt

As mentioned previously, malt, or malted barley, is one of the first ingredients worked into the production of beer. Its starches are converted into fermentable sugars during mashing, giving the yeast something to metabolize into alcohol, adding sweetness to the finished beer, and influencing head retention and color.

But before we can even think about brewing beer with barley, it must first be malted. In short, the malting process involves soaking the grain in water at 50°-65° Fahrenheit (for two to three days) and then allowing it to germinate (for six to ten days) at a temperature range of 50°-70°. This modifies insoluble starch chains to water-soluble starches, and activates proteolytic and diastatic enzymes into desirable mash components. Maltsters can control the degree of modification by the managing the length to which the acrospire, the first shoot of growth, is allowed to grow during germination. Once the grain reaches the desired modification, it is dried to prepare for the next step.

Malting complete, the grain is next kilned (roasted). Varying times and temperatures determine the finished product. British and American pale malts, which are frequently used as base malts, are kilned between 130° and 180°, while Munich malts are kilned at low temperatures before the malt has dried, and then the temperature is gradually raised to between 210° and 244°.

Crystal and caramel malts are fully modified during malting, and are kilned at 50 percent moisture content. The temperature is raised to between 150° and 170° and held for anywhere between one-and-a-half to two hours. This converts starches into sugars, creating malts that will later add sweetness to the finished beer. These malts are then kilned at a variety of temperatures to influence a desired color in the beer. Beer color is measured in degrees Lovibond (SRM).

The SRM scale moves from low to high, with a pale yellow American light lager registering in the neighborhood of 2-3 SRM, an amber ale landing around 10-17, and stouts clocking in at 30-40. The scale is a calculation based on the contributions of the grains involved, so it is possible for some stouts to rate much higher, though a 60 SRM Russian Imperial Stout is dark as night and is essentially black.

Chocolate and Black Patent malts are under-modified, and are kilned at high temperatures (420°-450°) to create an even darker hue while stunting the starches within. These malts offer coffee, chocolate and burnt notes in addition to dark color.

The author adds hops to a batch of beer at Rock Bottom Restaurant and Brewery in Des Moines.

Hops

Once the sweet wort is produced from water and malt, hops (either used as whole hops, pellets, plugs, or extracts) are added during the boiling phase of brewing to produce a number of desired effects. Bitterness, flavor and aroma are the three most readily noticed contributions of hops, but this cone-like flower also influences foam stand (the beer's head), helps with kettle coagulation, and acts as a natural preservative.

As mentioned previously, bittering additions happen in the early phase of the boil, followed by flavor and aroma additions, where appropriate. The level of bitterness pulled from the hops is influenced by the percentage of alpha acids in the hop. The essential oils present in the hop flower contribute flavor and aroma in the finished beer. The longer hops are present in the boil, the more their volatile oils flash away (hence the late additions to contribute these effects). Boiled longer, hops become increasingly water-soluble, locking in their bitterness.

Broadly speaking, there are three groups of hops: those of British origin, those hailing from Continental Europe and those from the United States (particularly the Pacific Northwest). English hops lean toward grassy, earthy, or woody characteristics. Continental hops carry a spicy, herbal bent. American hops are generally more brash, with higher alpha acid levels and stronger traits of pine and citrus.

Bitterness is measured in International Bittering Units. A light American lager logs in at 8-12 IBUs, while a double (or imperial) India pale ale (IPA) ranges between 60-120 IBUs (though the scale tops out at 100 and perceived bitterness can come from other factors, such as that Burton water profile mentioned previously).

Yeast

Though there are dozens of distinct beer styles, the whole lot can be broken down into two broad categories, ale and lager, thanks to the final essential beer ingredient, yeast. This magic ingredient is the unicellular microorganism hailing from the Saccharomyces genus, and the temperature at which either *Saccharomyces cerevisiae* (ale yeast) or *Saccharomyces carlsbergensis* (lager yeast) best performs during fermentation determines its grouping among beers.

Once the wort has been boiled, it is cooled rapidly to a suitable fermentation temperature, and yeast is pitched (introduced) to consume the fermentable sugars in the wort and converts it to alcohol and CO_2. Ale yeasts, known as top fermenting yeasts, function best at warmer temperatures (55°-75° Fahrenheit), while bottom fermenting lager yeasts perform optimally at cooler temperatures (46°-56° Fahrenheit).

In short, ales tend to have fruitier characteristics, while lagers tend to be crisper and cleaner on the palate.

As there are many different ale and lager yeasts in use, yeast choice for any given beer style is determined by the its specific characteristics, whether the ability to metabolize different sugars, survive in a higher alcohol environment, or the ability to flocculate, or settle out following fermentation to produce a clearer beer.

In addition to alcohol and CO_2, yeasts may also produce a number of by-products such as esters (fruity aromas), fusel alcohols (solvent), diacetyl (buttery), and sulfur (rotten eggs) compounds. In some beers, these by-products are acceptable and in other beers, they represent a clear flaw. Yeast health, sanitation and fermentation temperature, as well as choosing the right yeast for the right beer, influence these factors and are crucial to making quality beer.

But enough about how beer is made. Let's go find it.

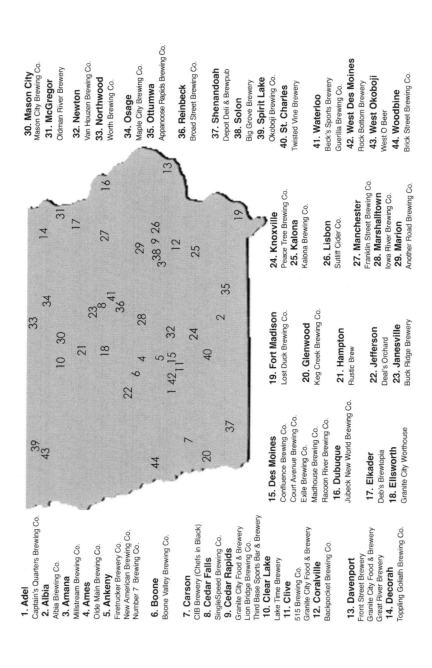

1. Adel
Captain's Quarters Brewing Co.

2. Albia
Albia Brewing Co.

3. Amana
Millstream Brewing Co.

4. Ames
Olde Main Brewing Co.

5. Ankeny
Firetrucker Brewery Co.
New American Brewing Co.
Number 7 Brewing Co.

6. Boone
Boone Valley Brewing Co.

7. Carson
CIB Brewery (Chefs in Black)

8. Cedar Falls
SingleSpeed Brewing Co.

9. Cedar Rapids
Granite City Food & Brewery
Lion Bridge Brewing Co.
Third Base Sports Bar & Brewery

10. Clear Lake
Lake Time Brewery

11. Clive
515 Brewing Co.
Granite City Food & Brewery

12. Coralville
Backpocket Brewing Co.

13. Davenport
Front Street Brewery
Granite City Food & Brewery
Great River Brewery

14. Decorah
Toppling Goliath Brewing Co.

15. Des Moines
Confluence Brewing Co.
Court Avenue Brewing Co.
Exile Brewing Co.
Madhouse Brewing Co.
Raccoon River Brewing Co.

16. Dubuque
Jubeck New World Brewing Co.

17. Elkader
Deb's Brewtopia

18. Ellsworth
Granite City Worthouse

19. Fort Madison
Lost Duck Brewing Co.

20. Glenwood
Keg Creek Brewing Co.

21. Hampton
Rustic Brew

22. Jefferson
Deal's Orchard

23. Janesville
Buck Ridge Brewery

24. Knoxville
Peace Tree Brewing Co.

25. Kalona
Kalona Brewing Co.

26. Lisbon
Sutliff Cider Co.

27. Manchester
Franklin Street Brewing Co.

28. Marshalltown
Iowa River Brewing Co.

29. Marion
Another Road Brewing Co.

30. Mason City
Mason City Brewing Co.

31. McGregor
Oldman River Brewery

32. Newton
Van Houzen Brewing Co.

33. Northwood
Worth Brewing Co.

34. Osage
Maple City Brewing Co.

35. Ottumwa
Appanoose Rapids Brewing Co.

36. Reinbeck
Broad Street Brewing Co.

37. Shenandoah
Depot Deli & Brewpub

38. Solon
Big Grove Brewery

39. Spirit Lake
Okoboji Brewing Co.

40. St. Charles
Twisted Vine Brewery

41. Waterloo
Beck's Sports Brewery
Guerilla Brewing Co.

42. West Des Moines
Rock Bottom Brewery

43. West Okoboji
West O Beer

44. Woodbine
Brick Street Brewing Co.

515 Brewing Company

Clive

It's Cinnamon Rost and Ariane Criger's fault. Looking to spend more time together, they introduced their husbands, Ryan and Brandon respectively, in hopes that their mutual interest in homebrewing would spark a friendship. That, it did, and with the addition of Dave Ropte and Bailey Forrest to the crew, the idea for 515 Brewing Company began to ferment.

Many gallons of beer later, the foursome opened the three-barrel nanobrewery at 7700 University Avenue in Clive. I happened to be there that day, and it was clear to me that folks in the Des Moines metro area were ready for a new local watering hole. A parched line of drinkers snaked out into the parking lot in advance of the doors' opening. Once unleashed, the crowd packed the taproom and drained 515's supply. The brewery started the day with seven beers on tap (plus a nitrogen-dispensed version of their imperial stout), and by the end of the night, stock remained for only three of their beers.

During my opening day visit, I tasted a spiced brown ale, a spiced Belgian pale ale, and a Berliner Weisse. All were solid. Word spread about the quality of the neighborhood brewhouse, and 515 has strained to keep up with demand, supplementing their offerings with guest taps from their Iowa brewery brethren.

The 515 foursome uses a small brewer's nimbleness to an exponential degree, and beers on offer rotate frequently. While they've shown skill in brewing styles throughout the spectrum, 515's OJ IPA (a wheat IPA) has become one of Iowa's most talked about IPAs. And it's not their only hop-leaning offering. OJ, which has more recently been transformed into a "session" IPA, is complemented by D.A.R.T. Dodger (a West Coast IPA) and Hopititis B (a double IPA), so hop heads have choices to keep them engaged.

While there are lots of choices, supply is always struggling to meet demand—515 is unable to offer growlers and has only been able to supply a handful of asked-for kegs to local bars for special occasions. Though brisk sales is a good problem to have, it still falls in the problem category, and 515 is working toward a solution. Fond of their taproom and its location on the Clive Greenbelt Trail, but without room to produce more beer, Bailey recently discussed plans to open a separate production facility, which will allow a steady supply of beer not only to the original taproom, but draught and bottle sales throughout the 515 area code for which the brewery is named.

For those who have tried the 515 lineup, this opening will be as anticipated as was the original start date, and I'm sure that Criger, Rost, Forrest and Ropte will have another big crowd to deal with. That should be no problem. They're getting used to it.

Trading kegs: Brian Sabus of Twisted Vine Brewing enjoys a laugh with 515 brewing Company's Bailey Forrest while making a keg delivery.

The Details

515 Brewing Company
7700 University Ave.
Clive, Iowa 50325
(515) 661-4615

Online: 515brewing.com, Facebook, Twitter
Owners: Brandon Criger, Ryan Rost, Bailey Forrest, and Dave Ropte
Brewmaster: Brewing duties shared by the owners
Year opened: 2013
Brewing system: 3-barrel
Tours: Yes
Availability: Taproom only
Parking: Free parking lot
Public Transportation: Bus stop within one mile; located within feet of the Clive Greenbelt Trail
Year-round beers: varies
Seasonal/limited release beers: varies
Food: Pretzels on site. Check social media for food truck availability. Patrons are welcome to bring food in.
Local non-beer attractions: Des Moines
Tip: Try the OJ IPA — its popularity is justified!

Notes:

Albia Brewing Company

Albia

In December of 2012, some thirty-two years after he brewed his first batch of beer, Brian Lindberg opened Albia Brewing Company (ABC) in his hometown. And he picked a beautiful location for it: Albia's historic Skean Block Building, which was built by Elmer Skean in 1889.

In its original incarnation, Skean Block housed a grocery store on one side and a shoe store on the other. As with many historic structures, it has hosted a laundry list of businesses, including a furniture store, funeral home, pool hall, clothing store and a bar or two. And it has also seen periods of vacancy. In 1996 the Bates Foundation acquired the property and proceeded with a $750,000 restoration, with a plan of making a home for a restaurant. Beautifully restored, Skean Block grabbed attention on Albia's already-quaint Historic Town Square, which boasts 92 buildings on the National Register of Historic Places. Eateries came and went, however, and the building sat empty for two years before Lindberg floated the idea of a brewpub. Though the Foundation had turned down a number of pitches, Albia Brewing Company received a green light.

Lindberg and his wife, Barb, bought the building, knocked a hole in an interior wall to link what would become the dining and pub sides of the establishment, and installed a five-barrel brewhouse with three fermenters upstairs and four brite tanks for conditioning in the basement. The brewhouse is on display behind glass on the east side of the building, which is set up for dining alone, while the west side of the space houses a five-seat bar and additional seating in a more bar-like environment. The structure is brick-and-wood beautiful with wall adornments leaning toward the history of Albia downstairs, while the upstairs meeting rooms—perfect for reunions, parties and conferences—feature period artwork. The exterior flashes Victorian, with original stained glass back in action after being discovered during the building's overhaul.

"I thought we'd have a pub, with a real active night life," Brian said. "But it morphed into a family place right away."

With a few tweaks to an essentially turnkey purchase, the Lindbergs opened their brewpub, serving an assortment of appetizers, salads, sandwiches, and specialty pizzas. I can't help but mention Brian's 50/50 Burger by name. Here's ABC's description: "Brian's unique blend of 50% prime beef and 50% bacon grilled to perfection, and topped with pepper jack cheese, avocado mash, and a sunny-side-up egg with chipotle adobo mayonnaise, lettuce, and tomato. Served on a Kaiser roll."

Though Brian talks up the pizzas, it's hard to consider ordering a pizza with a burger like that on the menu. And then there's the beer.

On my visit, Brian had eight of his own beers on tap: Soap Creek Shandy, Hops² Wheat, 1889 Red Ale, Avery Pale Ale, Cinnamon Apple (gluten-free), Coal Miner Bock,

Brian Lindberg of Albia Brewing Company takes a break in the brew house.

Dooley's Rye Porter, and Black Betty Milk Stout. He also had a house-made root beer and a trio of guest taps. And he pours a blend or two, as well, with his milk stout working well in combination with either cider or his house bock.

"I'm one of the luckiest guys in the world in all reality," Brian said, as he walked me through his brewpub. "Things do fall into place, but you've got to put the time and work and effort into it."

Brian is no stranger to work. A serial entrepreneur, he has an insurance agency, as well as a lodge and outfitting company for deer and turkey hunters. The hard work has paid off. With good crowds and patrons ranging in age from eight to 80, Albia Brewing Company has ably filled a number of gaps in Albia's business catalog. It's a brewery, it's a restaurant, and it's a community hangout.

The Details

Albia Brewing Company
11 Benton Avenue E
Albia, Iowa 52531
(641) 895-3224

Online: albiabrewingcompany.blogspot.com, Facebook, Yelp
Owners: Brian and Barbara Lindberg
Brewmaster: Brian Lindberg
Year opened: 2012
Brewing System: 5-barrel
Tours: Yes
Availability: draught only
Parking: Historic Albia Square
Year-round Beers: Avery Pale Ale, Coal Miner Bock Beer, 1889 Red Ale, Soap Creek Shandy
Seasonal/Limited Release Beers: Pumpkin, Octoberfest, Cinnamon Apple, bock and stout variations
Food: Pizza, sandwiches, appetizers, Wednesday specials (i.e.: Iowa chops, ribs, prime rib)
Local Attractions: Albia's Historic Square is listed on the National Historical District of Iowa; Iowa's largest weaving/yarn shop is located next door to the brewery, along with other shopping around the square; only 15 minutes away from Honey Creek Resort.
Tip: Come for the beer; stay for the 50/50 Burger.

Notes:

Another Road Brewing Company

Marion

When brothers-in-law Alex Zoll and Robert Rinehart married sisters Aryn and Emily Robison, they inherited most guys' dream father-in-law, the kind of guy that would propose starting a brewery. Attorney Jeff Robison brought the mutual love of beer of the quintet together to utilize unused space in the basement of his office building located at 1175 8th Avenue in Marion.

Operating under the belief that great beer is meant to be appreciated like great art, Another Road Brewing Company opened its doors in the late spring of 2014. Robert, who had been homebrewing with his father and brother for about seven years, jumped at the opportunity to snowball his hobby into a business, and he was tapped to head the brewing duties. Alex was lured back to Iowa from Colorado, where he'd been living for a number of years, to handle the business side of the project.

The brewhouse was up and running with a 10-gallon system on my visit just prior to opening, but the taproom was still under construction. A cozy space, the tasting area will seat about 30 thirsty patrons. Knowing the size of their rollout would stifle planned growth from the earliest of days, Robert and Alex had just ordered their 3-barrel brewhouse, which they hoped to bring online within a few months of opening. After a year or two establishing their brand, the Another Road crew plans to expand to a full-blown brewpub on the south side of Cedar Rapids, with yet another size upgrade.

In the meantime, customers can expect frequent beer rotations, with an IPA, hefeweizen, honey wheat, pale ale, porter, stout, and Belgian-styled beers in the works. Robert will also offer a house root beer and other sodas for kids and non-drinkers alike.

The Details

Another Road Brewing Company
1175 8th Avenue
Marion, Iowa 52302
(319) 212-8563

Online: anotherroadbrewing.com and Facebook
Owners: Jeff Robison, Alex Zoll, and Robert Rinehart
Brewmaster: Robert Rinehart
Year opened: 2014
Brewing System: 15-gallon, upgrading to a 3-barrel system
Tours: Yes

Parking: Lot, Street
Public Transportation: N/A
Year-round beers: Hayloft Hefe, Farmer's Daughter IPA, Bareback Belgian, Stone City Stout, Cheeky Queen Honey Wheat, Pale Ale
Seasonal/limited release beers: Constantly changing
Food: No, but deliveries are welcome
Local non-beer attractions: Bike trail, Uptown Marion shopping
Did you know? Another Road's name comes from a musical project that Jeff was involved in a number of years ago.

Notes:

Appanoose Rapids Brewing Company

Ottumwa

Owners Tim and Liz Ware weren't beer geeks when they took steps to open Appanoose Rapids Brewing Company in July of 2010—they were restaurateurs. During the planning stages of launching their dream, the Wares collaborated with a friend who suggested the brewpub angle to distinguish themselves from the competition.

Eventually, their friend pulled out of the partnership, but Tim and Liz decided to proceed with the beer angle. They rehabbed what morphed into a beautiful building in a ramshackle section of Main Street in Ottumwa. As it turned out, when they installed their modest 10-gallon brewing system, they were adding to the beery legacy of the 1875 structure. During the building's renovation, the Wares stumbled across a detailed tile mosaic hidden behind drywall and painted brown: Anheuser-Busch Beer. A little research, including a phone call or two to St. Louis, and Tim discovered that the building was once owned by Anheuser-Busch, most likely due to its proximity to the railroad, which is right out the back door. According to Tim, in the early 20th century, workers would roll 60-gallon wooden barrels of beer off the train and straight into the building, where they slaked thirst in an A-B "tied house" of sorts. The Wares kept the tile's historic nuance as well as some of the original flooring, and brought the building back to life after a dedicated year of hard work.

As Liz sorts out the brewhouse and the idiosyncrasies of the hardcore beer world, Tim holds down the kitchen, serving up fairly traditional American fare in a pleasant atmosphere. My visit revealed a trio of house beers—a blonde, a stout and a raspberry wheat—as well as 11 other taps, and a selection of bottled beers showing that Tim is unafraid of offering up mainstream lagers to widen his clientele. Tim said that the house beers rotate, with brown ales, pale ales, and riffs on wheat and fruited beers seeing tap time behind the bar.

Though it has functioned as a clothing store, grocery store, and a warehouse in previous lives, the entire dining room has been beautifully refurbished. With a charming, black back bar, punched tin ceilings, light fixtures packed with character, and red walls decorated with large-format, Liz-copied vintage beer advertisements from the likes of Marcellin Auzolle and Leonetto Cappiello, the brewpub has ample seating, in addition to a party room in the back.

With the help of a façade grant and a community initiative to restore a rather dilapidated section of town, Appanoose Rapids represents the start of a hopeful future for downtown Ottumwa.

The Details

Appanoose Rapids Brewing Company
332 E. Main Street
Ottumwa, Iowa 52501
(641) 684-4008

Online: appanooserapidsbrewingcompany.com, Facebook
Owners: Tim Ware
Brewmaster: Tim Ware
Year opened: 2010
Brewing system: 10-gallon
Tours: No
Availability: Onsite only
Parking: Yes
Year-round beers: Varies
Seasonal/limited release beers: Varies
Food: American
Did you know? The building housing Appanoose Rapids Brewing Company
   was once an Anheuser-Busch-owned pub.

Notes:

Backpocket Brewing Company

Coralville

One of the most enjoyable parts of being a beer lover is attending beer festivals, which are so prevalent across the country and around the world. And yes, we have them in Iowa, too. Beer fests are a great way to spend time with comrades, rub elbows with and learn from professional brewers, and explore new beers. It was at Millstream Brewing Company's Festival of Iowa Beers a few years ago, that I first became a fan of Brewmaster Jake Simmons' acumen.

At the time, he was brewing in McGregor's Old Man River Brewery, but he was in the process of extending his beers to other bars. With other Iowa beer drinkers responding to his German-inspired brewing style with the same enthusiasm that I did, building a larger production facility was soon on the agenda. What emerged was a new Iowa brewery, Backpocket Brewing Company, which Jake based in Coralville's Iowa River Landing Development to take advantage of the proximity to both Iowa City and Interstate 80. Though it was hardly an overnight project, Backpocket leapt to the front of the pack and became the largest brewery in Iowa with its 30-barrel brewhouse when it opened in 2012.

It is a fully-automated, state-of-the-art sight for a beer lover's sore eyes. "Fine-tuned control is why we did it," said Jake. "Consistency for one, but to be able to eliminate all manual variables and dial in specific changes to make the beer and give you ultimate control over your product."

A stickler for the details, Jake maintains an extensive quality control laboratory, which mirrors the one he worked at early in his brewing career when he cut his teeth at Schlafly Brewing Company in St. Louis, Missouri. Built for growth (and currently doing contract brewing for his old Schlafly friends who are experiencing their own capacity issues), Backpocket was also constructed with the environment in mind, utilizing many "green" principles such as a pre-mash hydration system to maximize mash efficiency, a vapor condenser to recapture energy used to heat water and boil the wort, and a China cap to reduce energy use during the boil.

The brewhouse has pumps, tanks, and everything else one would expect to see, but it also has a touch-screen panel that does what it's told—every single time. "It doesn't take the art out of making the beer," said Jake, a defense against those who might rail against automated processes. "If anything, it enhances it, because if you don't control something, then you're just guessing. If you don't control the exact specifications of what you're doing, then you'll have variation and you can't get the beer exactly where you want it to be. It really enhances the art of brewing, as opposed to taking anything away."

Some may disagree, but there's no disputing the consistency of Jake's beers. They are unswerving. And while he tends to brew lagers in a markedly German style, Jake does spread his wings and innovate without disengaging Reinheitsgebot, the German Purity Law of 1516 which allows only malt, hops, yeast, and water to be used in the brewing process. Aside from the occasional stout or IPA on tap at the brewery or featured at a festival, Jake offers one of my favorites: Wooden Nickel, a Scottish peated lager, as part of his bottled portfolio. Made with Pilsner, amber, peated and roasted malts and a schedule of German hops, it's a hybrid of German and Scottish ancestry that I'd consider one of the country's best under-the-radar beers, a compliment I'd also offer about both Jake and Backpocket.

Like many breweries, Backpocket offers a "mug club" for regular patrons.

The Details

Backpocket Brewing Company
903 Quarry Road
Coralville, Iowa 52241
(319) 466-4444

Online: backpocketbrewing.com; Facebook, Instagram, Untappd, and Twitter
Owners: Jake Simmons, Jim and Kathy Simmons, Dave and Marci Strutt
Brewmaster: Jake Simmons
Year opened: 2012
Brewing system: 33-barrel

Tours: Yes

Availability (packaging and distribution area): Statewide, excluding the
Mason City and Sioux City areas

Parking: Available in back of brewery, and in the parking ramp next to the Marriott

Public Transportation: Bus-Coralville Transit System

Awards received: "Best Brewery/Winery 2013" by Iowa City Press-Citizen;
"Best New Restaurant 2012" by Iowa City Press-Citizen

Year-round beers: Gold Coin (Helles), Slingshot (Dunkel), Penny Whistle
(Weizen), Wooden Nickel (Peated Bock), Jackknife (GPA)

Seasonal/limited release beers: Cane Blade DIPA, RAYGUN IPA,
Backsprocket Summer Session, Oktoberfest

Annual Events: Brrrfest (winter beer festival held generally last Saturday in January)

Food: Stone oven pizzas, including a bacon Nutella dessert pizza, and salads

Local non-beer attractions: University of Iowa football and basketball

Tip: For something completely different, try Backpocket's Wooden Nickel,
a hybrid beer recalling both Scottish and German beer elements.

Notes:

Beck's Sports Brewery
Waterloo

Located at 3295 University Avenue in Waterloo, Beck's Sports Brewery is a sprawling sports bar that is sure to have a beer to suit any Iowa sports fan's fancy, whether they follow the Iowa Hawkeyes, Iowa State Cyclones, University of Northern Iowa Panthers, or the local USHL hockey squad, the Waterloo Black Hawks.

Part of the Barmuda family of bars and restaurants, Beck's serves up Cy's Clone Ale, Hawkeye Golden Wheat, Panther Pale Ale, and Black Hawk Braxator to thirsty Waterloo sports fans. I sat at the upstairs bar so I could admire the copper brewhouse, which was visible through glass, while I sipped on the Braxator, my dark solution for a cold night in early February.

In addition to spacious upstairs bar, there was a raucous Saturday night crowd in the lower level of the establishment, making the most of the dance floor on "Country Night," as well as the progressive draws, which meant that in the 10 o'clock hour, I only paid $1.50 for my pint. Not bad, if you like country music. Unfortunately for me, I missed Retro Friday by 24 hours.

With televisions aplenty, Beck's would obviously be a good location to catch the big game with friends, but they've also got a pool room for those attuned to billiards, and a banquet room for larger private parties.

Though extreme beer nerds might feel out of place if they intend to geek out, Beck's offers low prices, a reputation for the best burger around, and HD jumbo screens for a well-rounded sports bar experience.

The Details

Beck's Sports Brewery
3295 University Ave.
Waterloo, Iowa 50701
(319) 234-4333

Online: barmuda.com
Owner: Darin Beck
Brewmaster: Jonathon Wolford
Year opened: 2000
Availability: On-site only
Parking: Street and parking lot
Year-round beers: Hawkeye Golden Wheat, Blackhawk Braxator, Panther Pale Ale, and Cy's Clone Ale
Seasonal/limited release beers: Ragin' Raspberry Wheat, Oktoberfest, and Buck's Light
Food: American traditional
Tip: For sports fans, Beck's is a great place to catch the big game.

Notes:

Big Grove Brewery

Solon

"It's an 800-square-foot slice of me doing whatever the hell I feel like doing," says Brewmaster Bill Heinrich of his 3.5-barrel playground. An IPA lover, Bill's job is to fuel the taps at Solon's Big Grove Brewery, and when I walked in the door for a visit, Bill was feeling like brewing an IPA, one of two he tries to have pouring at any given time.

In order to do that, Bill brews frequently—because his beers are popular—and as I tasted his wares, I found that he's more than a one-trick pony.

"If we try and pander (whether to a 'nerd market' or a light-beer crowd), we're going to get killed. Nobody's going to dig it. It has to be authentic or we're not going to get anywhere. Nobody's going to drink it, and so we might as well make what we like to drink, and somebody will dig it."

So far, customers seem to dig it. And IPAs are the soul of Bill's lineup. He went out west to study the IPA scene and returned with plans of contributing to it. Bill works to keep two of his own IPAs on tap, but also has hopes to produce a family of notable sour beers. Bill puts out toothsome offerings ranging stylistically from a Berliner Weisse and a nitro-poured dry stout to a barrel-aged imperial stout to something called the Red-Headed Stranger. That last one is a tribute to co-owner's Doug Goetsch's hero: Willie Nelson. It was a noteworthy red ale served appropriately in a willi glass and treated exclusively with Nelson Sauvin hops. While there were a number of obscure Willie references to the beer, no, there were no hemp seeds involved. I asked.

A former brewer at BJ's in Reno, Nevada and Millstream Brewing Company in Amana, Iowa, Bill has found that he's not the only hophead in the vicinity. And so brewing well-constructed examples of popular styles on a limited scale can cause him capacity issues. "Something clicks, and it's gone," says Bill. "Suddenly the IPA and the wheat will be down at the same time, and that's always embarrassing."

Making a name for itself for not only its beer but also its food, the brewery was originally planned to be an addition to Red's Alehouse in North Liberty, a noted beer bar in the area. But as the concept shaped up, it moved to a stand-alone location with ownership that included the mother-son combo of Faye and Matt Swift from Reds as well as Doug. Originally from the area, Doug brought a strong kitchen background to Big Grove.

While Bill holds down the brewhouse, Doug makes sure the restaurant side is up to snuff. Serving as the managing partner, Doug graduated from and worked at the Culinary Institute of America in Napa Valley, California. He tapped Chef Ben Smart from The Herbfarm outside Seattle. A local boy, Smart's first cooking gig was working for the Swifts at Sluggers. The move brought his career full circle. With a baking background, Ben bakes all of Big Grove's breads fresh on site.

Fresh. Homegrown. Authentic. These are the words that Doug tosses around as he elucidates on Big Grove's intent. "The whole idea behind all of this is to make good food, make good beer, and stay humble," he says. "We try to do everything we can from scratch, and put a little craftsmanship behind it to match the craftsmanship that goes into the beer."

Add a little hospitality—and a gorgeous two-ton burr oak bar milled by hand from a 150-year-old tree—and you've got Big Grove Brewing Company.

Nestled in the center of a triangle that allows a traveler to be in Iowa City, North Liberty and Cedar Rapids all within about 10 miles, Big Grove gives the beery traveler cause to make a stop in Solon. Folks are already making the trip, and Bill's happy for the work it gives him: "I've got a lot of brewing to do," he says. "And to be honest, it's way the heck better than accounting."

Bill Heinrich takes a gravity reading while brewing a batch of IPA.

The Details
Big Grove Brewery
101 W. Main Street
Solon, Iowa 52317
(319) 624-2337

Online: biggrovebrewery.com, Facebook
Year opened: 2013
Brewing system: 3.5-barrel
Tour: Yes
Availability: Onsite only
Parking: Street
Public Transportation: No
Awards received: 2013 Iowa City Press Citizen Best New Restaurant
Year-round beers: BGB IPA; Que Sera, Sera Berliner Weisse
Seasonal/limited release beers: Big Grove has/will be releasing some combination of stouts, bourbon barrel-aged Russian imperial stouts, single-hop showcase IPAs/Pales, DIPAs, sours/wild ales, porters, coffee porters, and whatever else Bill dreams up.
Food: American fare with an emphasis on local, fresh ingredients and quality preparation and service.
Tip: All of Big Grove's breads and stocks are made fresh, in-house.

Notes:

Boone Valley Brewing Company

Boone

I don't have a worthy excuse for the good folks at Boone Valley Brewing Company, but they'd been open for over a year before I tasted their beers. And it's not like the opportunity didn't present itself; I'd attended at least two festivals at which they were pouring their beers, but somehow wandered around like a three-year-old trying to navigate college. The end of the day came and went (twice!), and I failed to take the BVBC exam. Party foul.

Finally, I carved out a Saturday to redeem myself with trek to the two-barrel nano-brewery in Boone, and was I glad I did! Usually on my first visit to a new brewery, I order a sampler to assess the breadth of a brewer's talent, but when I walked into Boone Valley for my long-overdue first visit, I wasn't feeling pensive; I was feeling thirsty. Regrettably, I missed the Oktoberfest tapping by one day, so I ordered my old standby: stout. Denied. Waylaid by a thirsty clientele, the taproom was fresh out, and I had to deviate from my version of comfort food. Not a problem. I quenched my thirst with a pale ale, a worthy consolation prize brewed by Brewmaster Rick Srigley.

Rick and Jon Crook started homebrewing together after Jon and his wife Danielle (Rick's daughter) bought Rick a homebrewing kit for Christmas some 13 years ago. Rick ran with the hobby, while Jon soon learned that he was content to drink his father-in-law's creations. Rick and his son-in-law/business partner installed the brewery in what was a 1961-born bus stand for travelers passing through Boone. The location served other purposes, but during the buildout, the group found traces of the pre-1961 use of the place—it was a parking lot. And today you can still see parking places on the wall.

Brand-new interior décor complements the character of the building, and Rick's background as a finish carpenter was critical to creating a beautiful space on a budget. With a capacity of about 50, the taproom is pleasantly intimate, and between conversations with the bartenders (who wouldn't bend and pour me an Oktoberfest) and the kind lady sitting next to me at the bar, I completely ignored my beerdrinking sidekick. Fortunately, he too was good at occupying himself with Boone Valley's two best assets: beer and people.

Starting out on a one-barrel brewhouse, Rick has had no trouble pleasing palates with his brewing talent, and part of the Boone Valley plan was to pique interest, and then scale up. In March of 2014, the brewery purchased a property across the street, and began efforts to install a 20-barrel brewhouse, a farm of 40-barrel fermenters, and a bottling line which will allow them to expand much further into Iowa's thirsty hearts. In addition to the bigger brewhouse to kick up production, BVBC added a three-barrel pilot brewhouse for small batches for the taproom, special beers for bars, or private label beers for parties.

"We can get a good reach on a 20-barrel system," says Jon, who plans to outgrow that space within four or five years, and then build a larger production facility to cope with the growth they hope to encounter. In that case, the emerging 20-barrel facility could become a dedicated "sour house" to specialize in sour beers. Or not. "Who knows what we will do?" Jon says.

Though this new facility will be BVBC's introduction to grocery store shelves, it will not be their first bottle release. In 2013, they put out a limited release: 245 bottles of their Ol' Griz Barley Wine, which was well received after much anticipation from locals who tasted it right when the brewery opened. Rick signed and numbered bottles served as a thank-you to the brewery's supporters. "For us, it's a really expensive beer to make," says Jon. "We age it for a long time [prior to release], but we wanted to do something special with that first release."

The plan is to have the production facility up and running by August of 2014, and BVBC has a number of ideas fermenting away to make a splash, whether "everyday" beers, barrel-aged nuggets, or cider collaborations with a local winery.

"We're a brewery that is going to be concentrating on—I wouldn't say the cutting, bleeding edge weird stuff—but the fun stuff. I don't see us ever taking a bag of dough-nuts and throwing them into a fermenter," says Jon. "That's not really our cup of tea, but we might take something that's classical and put a twist on it, and do it right. We are picky with our beers, and put out quality stuff."

If the barrel-aged imperial red ale I tried on a recent visit is any indicator, the bottles coming out of Boone Valley will be attention-grabbers, and beer drinkers outside of Iowa will take notice—because Rick is doing something right.

The Details

Boone Valley Brewing Company
816 7th Street
Boone, Iowa 50036
(515) 432-1232

Online: boonevalleybrewing.com, Facebook
Owners: Jon Crook, Danielle Crook, and Rick Srigley
Brewmaster: Rick Srigley
Year opened: March 2012
Brewing system: 3-barrel
Tours: Yes
Availability: Tap room only. Growlers available. Bottles on the horizon.

Parking: street

Year-round beers: Roxie Irish Red, Iron Horse IPA, Midnight Stout, and Pintail
Pale Ale

Seasonal/limited release beers: Ol' Griz Barley Wine, English Mild, Dunkel-
weizen,
Hefeweizen, Imperial Irish Red, Vanilla Bourbon Imperial Porter,
and Blue-Eyed Brown

Annual events: BarleyWine release party in December

Food: No, but carry-in is welcome

Local non-beer attractions: Boone Scenic Valley Railroad, Seven Oaks Ski resort,
Boone Speedway, Bike Trails, and Honey Creek Golf Course

Tip: Boone Valley has some interesting beers for the future, but the oatmeal stout
won't steer you wrong while you wait.

Notes:

*Boone Valley's
Danielle Crook pours a
pint in the taproom.*

Brick Street Brewing Company

Woodbine

Brick Street Brewing Company faced the same dilemma that so many other new breweries have had lately. Anticipation. Popularity.

With a community celebration (Applefest) on the calendar and a license in hand green lighting production, brewer Justin Eilers set out to open the doors of his new one-barrel nanobrewery to take advantage of the 15,000 extra bodies in town for the festivities. And they wiped him out.

I was going to make a special trip—about 45 miles north of Omaha, Nebraska—on opening day in September of 2013 to get an early taste of Eilers' wares myself, but my schedule wouldn't permit it. Nearly a month later I made the trek. Brick Street Brewing Company, named for the beautiful historic downtown streets—part of the Lincoln Highway, which stretches from New York to San Francisco—was still struggling to meet demand on their small brewing system. I could see why.

The taproom is cozy, which is another word for small. But it's also cozy in a warm and comfortable way. If I lived nearby, I'd love having a quiet pint in this space. The bar is stainless steel, the floors are stained concrete, the walls carry a splash of yellow, and naked light bulbs add mood. It's not nice in the manner of a million-dollar renovation. It's nice in the way that it inspires me to go home and remodel my own man cave. It makes me believe that I could create a good drinking space on a nano budget and wow my friends.

I tasted two beers: You Don't Know Jack, a spiced pumpkin ale, and PK's Porter, a 4.9% porter simply packed with flavor. Justin's three fermenters were filled and working their little hearts out to help him take over the remaining real estate—six more tap handles being place-held on my visit with a variety of guest beers.

Turning pro after just four years of avid homebrewing, Justin has plans for a lot of seasonal rotation supplementing the "usual suspects" on the taplist (blonde, IPA, nut brown, etc.). And somewhere down the brick path, he hopes to start bottling. After tasting his porter and hearing this, I found myself agreeing with another Iowa brewer who had recently chatted with Justin and said, in parting, "You're going to want to buy my three-barrel brewhouse in about a year."

I ordered another sub-5% porter, nibbled on a slice of pizza I had ordered in and contemplated this statement. I decided that there's a good chance that he was right; a one-barrel brewing system wasn't nearly big enough for Brick Street's potential.

The Details

Brick Street Brewing Company
506 Walker St., Ste. B
Woodbine, Iowa 51579
(712) 592-1894

Online: brickstreetbrewing.com,
  Facebook, Twitter
Owners: Justin and Nicole Eilers
Brewmaster: Justin Eilers
Year opened: 2013
Brewing system: 1-barrel
Tours: Yes
Availability: Draught in the taproom and several locations in the region
Parking: Street
Year-round beers: Blonde Ale, Wheat, Pale Ale, IPA, Porter, and Stout
Seasonal/limited release beers: Summer Wheat (May-August), Apple Wheat
  (September-October), Pumpkin Spice Ale (October), Oktoberfest Lager
  (November-January), Winter Ale (December-February), Imperial (Double) IPA
  (May), Raspberry or Mango Wheat Ale (June-July), and Hoppy Wheat Ale
  (April)
Annual Events: Woodbine's Applefest
Food: Pub snacks initially, with possible limited menu to come
Local non-beer attractions: The scenic Loess Hills drive, Artisan Studio & Gallery,
  White's Floral Garden, the Zell Millard Historic Preservation Park which includes
  Merry Brook Rural School Museum, Harrison County Genealogy, the original
  Depot, and a CNW caboose, as well as a renovated 1928 canopy gas station.
  Woodbine and nearby towns also have many antique stores, specialty boutiques,
  and other unique shopping. Within less than an hour's drive are several other local
  breweries and wineries, including Breezy Hills in Minden, Keg Creek Brewing
  Company in Glenwood, and Prairie Hawk Vineyards & Winery in Council Bluffs.
Tip: At less than 5% ABV, Brick Street's porter is packed with flavor while
  remaining sessionable.

Notes:

Broad Street Brewing Company

Reinbeck

Walk inside the simple taproom of Reinbeck's Broad Street Brewing Company and you'll find hardwood floors, a small bar, and windows looking into the fermentation cellar. The wood-jacketed quartet of open fermenters, along with their matching seven-barrel brewhouse, offer a vintage look acquired from The Orange Brewery in London. There are but four seats at the cozy bar, and, on my visit, they were well-anchored by locals immersed in conversation.

My family took advantage of the cache of board games on the shelf while I sidetracked myself into a conversation with head brewer Craig Klinefelter. Craig and his stepson, owner/brewmaster Trevor Schellhorn, focus their brewing on English styles. On my visit, I tried the 175 Light Lager, Broad Street Wheat, Black Porter, Coo Coo Cachoo ESB, Vanilla Porter and Sticky Wickett, an American-hop driven pale ale. As if blessed by the British-sourced equipment on which they were brewed, the Brit-leaning ESB and both porters were particularly good. Though they were soft and drinkable pushed from a keg, Craig dropped the really good news: one or the other can often be found exclusively on cask at the Mucky Duck in Ames — a real treat and worth putting that stop on the radar for a future beer junket.

Trevor and Craig have a background in homebrewing that began when Trevor's then-girlfriend, now-wife, bought him a beer kit as a gift. Craig joined in, and some 15 years later when Craig retired from a career in the seed industry and Trevor exited his contracting trade, in 2011, Broad Street was born.

On draught only at the taproom and around 20 bars and restaurants in the area, Broad Street saw a 91 percent increase in sales from 2012-2013, and is hoping for a somewhat more manageable increase of 50 percent this year. Though they have four labels approved, their rapid growth has brought its own headaches, so while Craig has bottling on his to-do list, Broad Street is concentrating on managing demand for its present accounts and is in no hurry to put beers into bottles.

A real treat in a town of just over 1,600 residents, Broad Street is a nice Grundy County headquarters for a tasty beer, and plays host to pub quizzes, live music and an annual "Becktoberfest" celebration. And I can attest to the good that Broad Street can do to a Sunday afternoon, as well.

A group of locals partake at Reinbeck's Broad Street Brewing Company.

The Details

Broad Street Brewing Company
113 Broad Street
Reinbeck, Iowa 50669
(319) 350-0749

Online: broadstreetbrewing.com, Facebook
Owner/Brewmaster: Trevor Schellhorn
Year opened: 2011
Brewing System: 7-barrel
Tours: Yes
Availability: Draught only in the Waterloo/Cedar Falls/Marshalltown and
  surrounding areas
Year-round beers: Reinbecker Rye Ale, Black Porter, 175 America Lager,
  Coo Coo Cachoo ESB, Sticky Wickett PHB
Parking: Street
Tip: Broad Street specializes in English-style beers—check out the ESB or porter!

Notes:

Buck Ridge Brewery

Janesville

Though actively absorbing the taste and culture of the Colorado beer scene where he lived prior to returning to his native Iowa in 2007, it wasn't until Andrew Saucke stumbled across a wild hop field outside of Boulder that he immersed himself in brewing itself. He began brewing with the hops, which he named Boulder Wild, and transplanted rhizomes to begin growing them himself. On visits to Iowa, Andrew would bring samples of his creations to his father and family friend Jim Landau, the latter requesting that he'd like the beers on tap at his restaurants if ever Andrew's beers became commercially available.

Andrew eventually came home to live in Iowa to raise his family, and soon took steps to fulfill Landau's appeal. A full-time stay-at-home dad, he established the 10-gallon Buck Ridge Brewery to supply Landau's Montage and The Brown Bottle, both in Cedar Falls. And at present, these are the only two locations to find his beers, which are brewed almost exclusively with Andrew's homegrown hops, including his beloved Boulder Wild variety.

With interest from other potential accounts for his beer, Andrew is looking at adding fermentation space to increase his production. "We're small time, and I love what I'm doing," Andrew says of his nano operation that has been born out of the requests of others. "I can't fail."

But since he produces most of his own hops—especially his signature variety—Andrew plans to bank at least one more hop harvest before increasing his production. In addition to his hops, Andrew has raspberries and a new vineyard installed on his property, and so when the increase arrives, both beer-wine hybrids and raspberry-infused beers remain a possibility.

But Cedar Falls-area drinkers will have to wait and see what happens.

The Details

Notes:

Buck Ridge Brewery
8113 Buck Ridge
Janesville, Iowa 50647
(319) 885-4106

Owner/Brewmaster: Andrew Saucke
Year opened: 2011
Social Media: Facebook, Twitter
Brewhouse: 10-gallon
Availability: Buck Ridge brews exclusively for The Brown Bottle and Montage in Cedar Falls
Beers: Summer Honey Ale (Summer), Iowa Pale Ale (IPA) (Spring-Summer), and Scotch Ale (Fall/Winter)
Tip: This nano operation's beers can only be found at The Brown Bottle and Montage in Cedar Falls.

CIB Brewery (Chefs in Black)
Carson

They don't brew in a farmhouse, but the father-son owners of Chef's in Black Brewery, George and Alex Carlton, are definitely *farmhouse* in their style of brewing. The term recalls French and Belgian beers historically brewed (often in actual farmhouses) in Flanders and Wallonia—think saisons and bieres de garde for reference points. These "styles" of beer are the toughest to compartmentalize into a tidy box due to the wide variety of ingredients that was (and still is) used to produce them. Yeast selection, spices and brewers' whim leads to a family of beers often carrying wide profile variances. In earlier days, many would have been fairly low in alcohol content and were used to hydrate thirsty farmers in a time and place with unsafe drinking water. But some are higher in gravity, as well. Saisons tend to ferment at a higher temperature than other beers (above the 80 degree Fahrenheit realm) while a biere de garde ferments a little cooler (in the neighborhood of 60 degrees) and can actually be a hybrid of sorts, utilizing either a lager or an ale yeast and fermenting slightly outside the comfort zone for each yeast. Either way, its color can range from blonde to quite dark and leans smooth and malty after a fair swath of time in the tank.

Of course, one needn't brew in a Belgian garage to produce a farmhouse-style ale. Many American craft breweries, including CIB, brew in this style. To produce their unique stable of beers, the Carltons utilize proprietary yeast blends, which include brettanomyces, lactobacillus and other wild yeasts. The result is perhaps the most unique lineup in the state—CIB beers are big, yeast-driven, complex, and lean toward sour. They add nuance with ingredients like coffee, oak staves, cherries and chili peppers. But the yeast is always the main attraction. I once told Alex that the CIB family of beers reminded me of the wild plums growing in the ditch south of my home. He took the fruit-tannin-funk description as the compliment that it was, noting that it meant *terroir*, something the CIB beers have over most breweries—and not just within the state of Iowa.

In 2011, George and Alex started out brewing 50-gallon batches on a home-built system in the basement of a ramshackle Main Street building in tiny Carson, home of but 812 residents. In 2013, the Carltons' 750-milliliter bottles were selling so well in Des Moines, Iowa City, Kansas City and Omaha that they committed to expansion. They bought a building across the street, moved up to a three-barrel brewing system, and are still in the process of building out a taproom so that sour beer enthusiasts can taste the CIB lineup right at the source. At the time of this printing, they were planning on opening the taproom in August of 2014.

Alex Carlton shares an unlabeled experimental beer with colleagues at a beer festival.

The Details

CIB Brewery
116 Broadway
Carson, Iowa 51525
(515) 450-2981

Online: CIBbrewery.com, Facebook, Twitter
Owners: George Carlton and Alex Carlton
Brewmaster: George Carlton
Year opened: 2011
Brewing system: 55-gallon
Tours: Yes
Availability: 750-mililiter bottles and draught available in Iowa, Nebraska, and Missouri
Parking: Street
Year-round beers: Dethhanger Quad Brown, Morningwood Sour Breakfast Ale, Cheri Tart, and Orange Scorpion
Seasonal/limited release beers: Purple, The Countess, and John's Sour Ale
Food: BBQ coming in 2014
Local non-beer attractions: Tubing on the Nishnabotna River, Carson Rodeo
Did you know?: CIB cultivates all their own yeast, lending funk and *terroir* to their beers.

Notes:

Confluence Brewing Company

Des Moines

Though there had been good, local beer on offer in Des Moines for over a decade, it wasn't until October of 2012 when homebrewers-turned-pro John Martin and Ken Broadhead opened Confluence Brewing Company that a production brewery came into the mix.

Located on the south side of Gray's Lake and named for the confluence of the Des Moines and Raccoon Rivers, CBC's 20-barrel brewhouse, helmed by Martin, cranks out a core of three flagship beers, Farmer John's Multi-Grain Ale, Des Moines IPA, and Capital Gold Lager (later adding the Thomas Beck Black IPA), as well as a slither of limited release beers ranging from a red lager to an oatmeal stout to a winter bock.

Coming out of the gates, they planned on launching cans in the spring of 2013, but their first anniversary rolled around and—guess what?—no cans on the shelves. Why? Too darned busy. This is something that a lot of folks don't understand about these small breweries. Judging by the posts on Facebook and Twitter, the casual observer might think that the brewers and brewery employees simply drink, cycle, sign books and goof off all day. Not so, and Confluence Brewing Company in Des Moines is a prime example of all the work that goes into operating a brewery.

There's an immense amount of work to be done. A lot of times in the early days, it's one or two or three individuals doing the work of six or eight or ten individuals—sometimes while maintaining another job. For John and Ken, demand exceeded their expectations by a long shot, and it was all they could do to keep the taps flowing.

"I know people want to be able to buy our beer in cans, and we want to deliver, but we want to do it in a very planned, organized manner that respects the integrity of our product," says John, who heads up duties in the brewhouse. "We originally purchased a two-head filler and single-head seamer." The pair intended to tiptoe into canning, before moving to a larger, more automated system. But it quickly became clear that this wouldn't work, given the support they found for their initial trio of beers. "The output of this system is somewhat limited and labor intensive," says John. "It became apparent that the small system would not meet our needs for very long."

But upgrading to the bigger canning line, not to mention additional tank space to support the endeavor, would mean a significant capital investment.

Smart, talented, and possessing the attention to detail reflected in the quality of his beers, John's former life as a project manager is shining through in his approach to

Confluence. So the cans are on hold, because they want to do it right. And besides, there's plenty of other work.

One of the business elements that caught them off-guard is the success of their taproom. "We still plan to can, but we want to make sure that we are ready for some increased growth as soon as we do. Our alternate plan for now is to continue to sell our 32 oz. Boston round growlers to retail accounts such as John's Grocery, New Pioneer Food Coops, Hy-Vee Wine and Spirits, etc. This gives the consumer a take-home package and lets us continue to grow our business at a reasonable pace," says John.

In the beginning, John and Ken, the latter keeping his full-time job for now, figured on doing most of the work themselves. Success has changed that. John's wife, Katie, deals with the bookkeeping, and demand has forced the hiring of a taproom manager, assistant brewer, sales rep, delivery driver, and about eight bartenders to staff the taproom.

"We appreciate the State of Iowa giving us the privilege to self-distribute our beer," says John. "At the relatively low volume we sell (compared to the major national brands), we count on the margin that we keep by distributing ourselves."

While Confluence is pleased to have some 90 accounts in the Des Moines metropolitan area, the taproom remains a big part of the brewery's magic. "The taproom has done so much better than planned. I think I hoped for this kind of success, but didn't plan on it in our business plan," John said. "I love that people can come to our production facility, in all its warehousey glory, and enjoy our beer at the point of origin."

Enter on the south side of building on Thomas Beck Road to have a walk-by mini tour of the brewhouse, or approach from the bike trail on the south side of Gray's Lake for quick access to the pleasant family of beers on offer. Either way, you will be pleased, likely departing with a growler of John's good stuff. Eventually, the cans will come. Eventually.

The Details

Confluence Brewing Company
1235 Thomas Beck Road, Suite A
Des Moines, Iowa 50315
(515) 285-9005

Online: confluencebrewing.com, Facebook, Twitter
Owner/Brewmaster: John Martin
Year opened: 2012
Brewing system: 20-barrel
Tours: Yes
Availability: Draught and 32 oz. Boston round half growlers in the Des Moines Metro, Ames, Iowa City and Cedar Rapids
Parking: lot, with overflow to the west
Public Transportation: Yes

Year-round beers: Des Moines IPA, Farmer John's Multi-grain Ale; Capital Gold Lager, Thomas Beck Black IPA

Seasonal/limited release beers: Small Town Brown, Mayday Maibock, ChewBOCKa Winter Bock, Blue Corn Lager, South Side Citra Blonde, Oktoberfest, East Side Attitude Red Lager, Gray's Lake Nessie Scottish Ale, Imogene Red Irish Ale, Takedown Irish Stout, Barley and Me Puppy Pale Ale, Rotating Pale/Amber Ale, Campfire Black Lager, High Water Oatmeal Stout,

Annual Events: Fall Fest (mid- to late-September)

Food: No, but you are welcome to bring in food and eat it in the taproom; occasional food trucks or food vendors, which is somewhat seasonal and is constantly developing. During the spring, summer, and fall plan on food vendors on Thursday, Friday, and Saturday.

Local non-beer attractions: Gray's Lake Park, Downtown Des Moines, Papa John Sculpture Garden

Tip: All of John's beers are good, but you really gotta try his Oktoberfest in the fall!

The brewhouse at Confluence Brewing Company in Des Moines.

Notes:

Court Avenue Restaurant and Brewing Company
Des Moines

Located in the Historic Court Avenue District in downtown Des Moines, Court Avenue Restaurant & Brewing Company (CABCo) opened its doors in 1996, following a three-year flood-induced vacancy of The Saddlery Building, which was built in 1881 by Muscatine, Iowa's J. Rubelman.

As the name suggests, Rubelman ran a saddle, harness and leatherworks in the space to take advantage of Des Moines' two rivers and 13 railways. He ran a successful trade for nearly 20 years. Before CABCo came along, the building housed a shoemaker, rubber company, stove manufacturer, glove company, as well as the Krispy Kone Company and the Kaplan Hat Company, the latter serving as both the name of a haberdashery and a restaurant. The building was listed on National Register of Historic Places in 1985.

The beer names—and label-geared art adorning the pubby walls—hearken back to an earlier time in Iowa's brewing history, with some named for defunct beers (Pointer Brown and Blackhawk Stout), while others suggest a similar sensibility (Two Rivers Light) or lean toward the latter with a little judicial sprinkling (Honest Lawyer IPA) to pay homage to the "neighborhood business," nearby (the Polk County Court House is but a block and a half to the west).

Brewmaster Justin Cloke entered the seven-barrel brewhouse in March of 2014, putting out five core brews (those mentioned above plus a Belgian white ale), as well as a rotating assortment of seasonal and reserve beers (not to mention a guest tap). Transitioning from homebrewer status to the realm of professional brewing after ditching the insurance industry for a stint at America's oldest brewing school, Chicago's Siebel Institute of Technology, Cloke's offerings are stylistically diverse, with his "regulars" complementing a wide array of seasonal and barrel-aged beers that he looks forward to exploring moving forward.

CABCo is walkable to the Wells Fargo Arena, the Civic Center of Greater Des Moines, the Science Center of Iowa and Blank IMAX Dome Theater, and Principal Park (CABCo pours an exclusive beer for the I-Cubs games), among other downtown attractions. Walk out the brewpub's front door on a Saturday morning in the summertime, and be you'll immersed in one of the country's biggest farmers markets. Visiting in the wintertime? No problem. You don't have to face the weather, as The Saddlery Building is accessible via Des Moines' climate-controlled Skywalk, a four-mile elevated walkway connecting restaurants, hotels, meeting facilities, shopping and more.

With a solid beer lineup and tasty menu (and homemade root beer and ginger beer for the kids), CABCo is a highlight of the attractive and pedestrian-friendly Court District.

Court Avenue Brewing Company in Des Moines offers a wide array of house brewed beers, as well as a full bar for spirits drinkers.

The Details

Court Avenue Restaurant and Brewery
309 Court Avenue
Des Moines, Iowa 50309
(515) 282-2739

Online: CourtAveBrew.com, Facebook, Twitter
Owners: Scott Carlson and Lloyd Linn
Brewmaster: Justin Cloke
Year opened: 1996
Brewing system: 7-barrel
Tours: Yes
Availability: On-site and draught beer available at the Iowa Cubs ball park, the Des Moines Arts Fest, the Iowa Craft Beer Tent at the Iowa State Fair, and at select local bars and restaurants.
Parking: Metered street parking, pay lots and garages are all nearby
Public Transportation: Des Moines Area Regional Transit Authority routes nearby, and the building is connected to the downtown Skywalk

Awards: Restaurant of the Year (Iowa Restaurant Association Beef Council), Four Stars Highly Recommended (Datebook), Good Neighbor Award (National Restaurant Association), Gold, Silver & Bronze (Festival of Wood & Barrel Aged Beer), Four Stars Certificate of Excellence (TripAdvisor), #1 Microbrewery (Cityview Magazine Des Moines Register)

Year-round beers: Two Rivers Light, Belgian White, Pointer Brown, BlackHawk Stout, and 21st Amendment Ale; Non-Alcoholic: Zimmerman's Root Beer and Wertzberger's Ginger Beer

Seasonal/limited release beers: In addition to core beers, CABCo always has at minimum a seasonal and a Reserve beer on tap

Annual events: Relays street party held the Friday of Drake Relays on Court Avenue between 3rd & 4th Streets

Food: Open seven days a week for lunch and dinner with a full array of eclectic food options made from scratch, using the freshest local ingredients when possible

Local non-beer attractions: Science Center of Iowa, State Capitol, Gray's Lake, Sculpture Garden, Governor's Mansion, Salisbury House and Gardens, Iowa State Fair, Downtown Farmer's Market, Downtown Riverwalk

Tip: Court Avenue brews a special beer, Iowa Oaks Ale, which you can enjoy at Principal Park during Iowa Cubs games.

Notes:

Captain's Quarters Brewing

Adel

Starting a brewery wasn't a part of the plan when Dave and Brenda Peshel bought a bar and opened Captain's Quarters in Adel in May of 2011, but when they started remodeling the upstairs apartment it suddenly occurred to them that rather than renovate it and enter the landlord business, they should convert the space to a small brewery to add value to their bar and pull an enjoyable long-term hobby into the business model. "It just seemed like the right thing to do," says Brenda. "I didn't want to be a landlord."

The Peshels had been brewing for 20 years, and utilized that experience to launch CQ Brewing in 2013. Brewing on a 50-hectoliter system, CQ batches yield about 10 gallons a pop, and they use the small system once a week to add dimension to their affinity for providing variety to their patrons. Brenda says that though CQ's Red IPA was extremely popular and is sure to return on a regular basis, the Peshels intend to use the brewery to introduce new beers and new styles on a consistent basis.

Captain's Quarters/CQ Brewing is nautically-themed, with décor ranging from pirates to Navy SEALs. The bar boasts 12 taps and over 130 different choices of beer in bottles, and Brenda makes it a point to keep the choices fresh in the bar, always bringing in something new for patrons to explore. Outside, CQ has a patio for alfresco drinking, and if you bring your own groceries, you're more than welcome to fire up the grill for a little barside picnic.

On my visit, the upstairs renovation wasn't complete, but the tile flooring provides a nice foundation to the space, which will include its own bar, extend CQ's seating, and be available for special parties and events. While there, take a moment to soak in the beautiful view of the Dallas County Courthouse directly across the street.

CQ is a family-owned business, with cross-training meaning that Dave, Brenda, or their son Dalton could be responsible for brewing your beer, pouring your beer, or mopping the floor on any given day. In only three years, Captain's Quarters has done its part to add nuance to the town of 3,600, which has seen growth of late. For the Peshels, variety is the draw, whether from their own brewery or from those they support in their endeavor to bring better beer to Iowa.

The Details

CQ Brewing
807 Main Street
Adel, Iowa 50003
(515) 993-4417

Online: cqbrewing.com, Facebook
Owners: Dave and Brenda Peshel
Brewmasters: Dave and Dalton Peshel
Year opened: 2011
Brewing system: 10-gallon
Tours: Yes
Availability: Only available on-site
Parking: Street
Year-round beers: All beers rotate on brewers' whim
Food: No, but carry-ins are welcome
Local non-beer attractions: Adel Sweet Corn Festival
Tip: While you're visiting the square in Adel, pay a visit to Al Dente Toffee for an unexpected sweet treat in a beautiful setting.

Notes:

Deal's Orchard

Jefferson

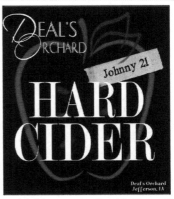

Frank Deal moved from Illinois to Jefferson, Iowa in 1917, and promptly planted, with the help of his sons Forrest and Lynn, 16 acres of apple trees to add to an existing orchard on his property. Narrowly escaping the 1940 Armistice Day freeze, the hobby turned into a family business over the years. In 1941, Forrest and Lynn replaced and expanded the depleted orchard, and today, the fourth generation of the Deal family is making its mark on the operation.

Benji joined the orchard in 2010, working with his parents, Jerald (Forrest's son) and Cindy Deal. A former high school math teacher, Benji has been in charge of hard cider development and production, and 2011 was the first year that the Deal family offered hard cider alongside their existing array of products.

With 45 acres of apple trees and over 25 varieties, apples are the primary focus, but the Deals start their retail season with sweet corn in July. The orchard sells tomatoes, sweet corn, apples, cider, gifts, Christmas trees, and much more from their diversified family farm. Once the Christmas tree season has passed, Deal's Orchard closes its Apple Barn gift shop.

Producing 750-1,000 gallons per year, Benji has only produced one hard cider product since he started, but in 2014, he hopes to expand into perry (pear cider). Available at the orchard as well as a few stores in Jefferson, Ames, and Carroll in 22-ounce bottles, the small production runs make a good excuse to head to the Jefferson area to find the refreshing drink right at the source. However, Benji is working toward expanding his footprint into the Des Moines area in the 2014 season.

While hard cider is a motivator to visit Deal's Orchard for those ticking Iowa breweries and cideries off their list, Deal's is a destination that is fun for the whole family. The orchard has hayrides, a corn maze, you-pick apples, and a wide array of children's entertainment that will make for a great day's fun for all.

The Details

Deal's Orchard
1102 244th Street
Jefferson, IA 50129
(515) 386-8279

Online: dealsorchard.com, Facebook
Owners: Jerald and Cindy Deal
Cidermaker: Benji Deal
Year opened: 1941
Tours: Orchard, yes; cider production area, no
Availability: Currently available onsite and in Jefferson, Ames, and Carroll at Fareways and Hy-Vees. Expansion to Des Moines area in 2014.
Parking: Parking lot
Annual event: Fall Festival
Food: Hot dogs, hamburgers, apple pie, apple dumplings, and dougnuts
Local non-cider attractions: Mahany Bell Tower
Tip: Several tour buses stop at Deal's Orchard each year.

Notes:

Deb's Brewtopia

Elkader

Passionate homebrewer/winemaker Deb Winter opened the first brewery in Elkader in 127 years when she launched the brewing wing of Deb's Brewtopia in September of 2013. Her 10-gallon brewing system served as an exciting addition to the homebrew shop that first opened a year earlier.

Servicing a handful of local bars and restaurants, and selling growlers on-site, the pressure on Deb's small setup soon became apparent. She recently sized up to a 30-gallon brewhouse to help meet the local demand for her beers, which include the likes of a rye IPA, an ESB, an Irish red ale, a hazelnut brown ale, an American wheat, and a German hefeweizen, as well as a sweet oatmeal stout (with riffs to keep things interesting).

An active part of the local homebrew club, the Turkey River Utopian Brewers, Deb is an indispensable local source of knowledge and support—and not simply because she peddles beer and winemaking ingredients and equipment.

But Deb's Brewtopia is about more than just beer ingredients. It's also about beer. Whether you're in the neighborhood for the area's many outdoor recreation opportunities or to catch a performance at the restored Elkader Opera House, stop by and pick up a growler of Deb's wares.

The Details

Notes:

Deb's Brewtopia
106 Cedar Street NW
Elkader, Iowa 52043
(855) 210-3737

Online: debsbrewtopia.com, Facebook
Owner/Brewmaster: Deb Winter
Year opened: 2012
Brewing system: 1-barrel
Tours: No
Availability: Draught, growlers
Parking: Street
Year-round beers: Rye IPA, ESB, Irish Red, Hazelnut Brown, Sweet Oatmeal Stout
with different variations, American Wheat, Hefeweizen, and American Wheat
Food: No
Local non-beer attractions: Elkader Opera House, white water project in Elkader,
canoe, kayak, tube rentals, and camping
Tip: You can purchase growlers of Deb's beer to consume off-site.

Depot Deli Restaurant and Brewpub

Shenandoah

Brewer/owner Bill Hillman of Shenandoah's Depot Deli and Lounge will tell you that beer is secondary, but his short list of beers do differentiate the restaurant he's owned for over thirty years from other small town diners in Southwest Iowa.

"I've got a weakness for old buildings," Bill said. He bought the railroad-side location and opened the deli in 1983 to prevent it from being demolished. With hand-breaded tenderloins and at least 10 homemade pies on offer at any time, Bill has pleased local diners while contributing heavily to the community. In addition to the Deli, he's had a hand in the development of the Wabash Trace Nature Trail, the restorations of several local buildings (Wabash Depot, The Dome, The Izaak Walton Lodge, and the Red Oak Firehouse, among others) as well as serving as the local chamber of commerce president.

Take a look around and you'll find a bombast of décor, with photos of Bill with everyone from Bill Clinton to the Everly Brothers (hometown boys) sprinkled on the walls amidst other bric-a-brac telling the story of a rural Iowa community.

The Depot Deli is a hub of local activity, serving breakfast, lunch and dinner every day of the year except Memorial Day and Labor Day. Bill hosts live music and organizes bike rides to Imogene each Tuesday, weather permitting. In September of 2012, Bill helped launch the Malvern-to-Shenandoah Marathon. Across the street from the Deli, you'll find one of the Everly Brothers' childhood homes on display (yep, Bill was involved).

Hillman added an extract brewhouse in 1996 to add interest. His Bill's Bock is his most popular offering and is always on tap, while two or three other styles rotate in and out. On a recent visit, the bock, which Bill brews with an ale yeast, was joined by a wheat beer, an IPA, as well as a blend of the bock and IPA named Katie, after Bill's daughter who can be found onsite waiting tables and slinging beers.

It goes without saying that I asked Katie to bring me a piece of pie. She happily obliged, and if you find yourself checking out Shenandoah's beer scene, I'd recommend that you save room for dessert.

The Details

Depot Deli Restaurant and Brewpub
101 Railroad Avenue
Shenandoah, Iowa 51601
(712) 246-4444

Online: depotdeli.com, Facebook
Owner/Brewmaster: Bill Hillman
Year opened: 1983 (restaurant); 1996 (brewhouse)
Brewing system: 10-Barrel
Tours: Yes
Availability: On-site only
Parking: street and parking lot
Year-Round Beers: Whistle Stop Wheat, Bill's Bock and Red Ale Blend
Events: RAGBREW (homebrew competition/Wabash Trace fundraiser), bike rides, live music, annual town celebration, annual marathon
Seasonal/Limited Release Beer: beers rotate at brewer's whim
Food: Full menu for breakfast, lunch and dinner (American)
Local non-beer attractions: Wabash Trace Nature Trail, Everly Brothers Boyhood Home
Tip: Save room for pie.

Notes:

Exile Brewing Company
Des Moines

"It's a tribute to my grandfather," said RJ Tursi of the name of the Des Moines brewery, Exile Brewing Company, which he and his family opened in August of 2012. "He gave us the opportunity to throw our hat into the ring in America, where you can actually make things happen, where there are opportunities out there to grab."

Grab opportunity, the Tursis have.

RJ's father, Bob Tursi, established the Latin King in 1983 at the age of 21, and found success in the restaurant while thinking back to his days of driving a beer delivery truck in his younger days. When RJ graduated with a finance degree but reticence to enter the field right away, Bob suggested a stint learning the winemaking business in Italy, where extended family operated a winery. RJ acted on the advice, and in Italy, fell in love with not only winemaking, but the process of fermentation.

RJ returned to Iowa, a questionable place to succeed in the wine business he surmised, and shifted focus to beer and brewing. Father and son built a small brewery in the garage. As the craft brewing business matured, the idea of opening a brewery emerged. After research and business planning, Exile Brewing Company was the name that surfaced to honor Joe Tursi and all the other immigrants who left their motherland for a new beginning. The émigrés referred to the Statue of Liberty as the "Mother of Exiles," and Joe spoke often of the day he arrived in New York, and what that torch-bearing statue meant.

Located at 1514 Walnut Street in downtown Des Moines, Exile Brewing Company possesses more than just a name to recall the Mother of Exiles—a local artist installed an exact copper-and-steel replica of her crown on the southeast corner of the building just two months after the brewery's opening.

"It's a statement on our permanence," said Tursi of the crown. "We feel like the equity in the crown is only going to grow."

Though the new Des Moines landmark has garnered much attention, it might seem a superfluous expense in the high-priced world of brewery start-ups. However, the lager-focused beers crafted by Brewmaster John Woodford offer a staying power all their own and the combination, along with a beautiful industrial drinking atmosphere, a beer garden, and kitchen offerings like a braised pork belly gyro (my go-to choice) will surely establish this brewery as a Des Moines must-visit for beer tourists.

With draught sales pushing the capacity limits of Exile's tank space, the 30-barrel brewhouse is working to expand with more fermenters, and will soon begin bottling three beers, Hannah (Bavarian wheat), Ruthie (gold lager) and GiGi (dark lager). Strong sales have always been considered a good problem to have, and one that Joe, the original exile, would be happy to see his grandson battle.

The Details

Exile Brewing Company
1514 Walnut Street
Des Moines, Iowa 50309
(515) 883-2337

Online: exilebrewing.com, Facebook, Twitter
Owners: Bob Tursi, RJ Tursi
Brewmaster: John Woodford
Year opened: 2012
Tours: Yes
Availability: On draught onsite and around the Des Moines area; bottles coming soon.
Parking: Street, lot
Year-round beers: Hannah Bavarian Wheat, Betty Honey Lager, Ruthie Gold Lager, and GiGi Dark Lager
Seasonal/limited release beers: Schwarzbier, German Pilsner, New Zealand Pale Lager, Maibock, Czech Pilsner, Kolsch-style Ale, Dark Chocolate Cherry Wheat, Rauchbier, and Oktoberfest
Food: A wide assortment of sophisticated pub-fare
Local, non-beer attractions: Science Center of Iowa, Blank Park Zoo, Des Moines Farmers Market, Brenton Skating Plaza, live music, shopping, and more.
Tip: Three words: pork belly gyro.

Exile Brewing's RJ Tursi showcases his beers at a beer festival.

Notes:

Firetrucker Brewery
Ankeny

Firetrucker Brewery in Ankeny is the brain-child of Dan Heiderscheit, Scott Kaven, and Neil Zaugg. The three homebrewers-turned-pro met a few years ago and quickly became friends, feeding off each other's brewing prowess and creative energy. They soon hatched a plan to start a brewery in Ankeny. "This is almost your quintessential home-brewer's dream come true," says Neil. "It's kind of a matter of us dreaming big and making it come true."

Dream big, they have. While many of the newer Iowa breweries are nano in scale, three-barrel brewhouses and smaller, Firetrucker dived right in with a 20-barrel brew-house and an ambitious plan. Though the threesome intends to start by servicing draught accounts close to home in Ankeny and the Des Moines area, they plan to be available statewide within five years and to grow to a regional contender within 10 years.

"The competition is forcing people to step up their game," says Dan, who is heading up the brewing duties and is looking forward to putting his beers into the hands of Iowa's increasingly savvy beer consumers. The entire Firetrucker concept is tied to-gether by the home they acquired. Housed in a former fire station on SW Third Street, the brewery's name, logo and even the beers possess fiery elements. Is it a coincidence that Dan has been smoking his own grains for use in his recipes for the past five years? Perhaps not. With Dan's delicate touch, smoky nuances will make occasional appear-ances in his beers to add aromatic and flavorful elements that tie into the branding.

In addition to a sharp logo and tasty beers, there's more art in store for followers of Firetrucker. "One of the goals is to keep the art and music and local connection part of the brewery," says Dan. "We want to create a good sense of community."

To do so, Dan, Neil, and Scott have plans to fill their space with more art than simply the stuff that brewers pour into glasses. Live music and art shows will be commonplace in the beautiful taproom, which boasts multiple seating areas to provide both bustle and privacy for thirsty patrons. The brewhouse is on display behind the custom-made black walnut bar. Ideally suited adjacent to the upcoming Ankeny Market and Pavilion Park (AMPK), the beer garden outside is visible not only to the AMPK, but also to the High Trestle Trail, thanks to a giant Firetrucker logo on the north side of the brewery's outbuilding. Southbound bikers will hear the siren's call, to be sure. And the Firetrucker guys have thought of everything, as there is plenty of bike parking, USB charging ports for phones and other electronic devices, and a parking space reserved for food trucks.

Firetrucker hopes to package beer in cans within a couple years of their June 2014 opening, and the packaging format will be a welcome addition to those next door at the AMPK.

With the personalities and skill sets to balance each other out, as well as a beautiful facility and comprehensive plan, Firetrucker Brewery is sure to garner attention within Iowa's beer community.

The Details

Firetrucker Brewery
716 SW Third Street
Ankeny, Iowa 50023
(515) 984-8060

Online: firetrucker.com, Facebook, Instagram, and Pinterest
Owners: Dan Heiderscheit, Scott Kaven, and Neil Zaugg
Brewmaster: Dan Heiderscheit
Year opened: 2014
Brewing system: 20-barrel
Tours: Yes
Availability: Central Iowa
Parking: Parking lot on north side of building shared with the Ankeny Market & Pavilion and on 3rd street.
Public Transportation: The Des Moines Area Regional Transit (DART) bus system provides daily connections for Ankeny with the rest of the metro area.
Year-round beers: Steam Engine California Common, House IPA, Burnout Brown, Black Bear Porter, and 2 Alarm Red.
Annual events: AMP Fest, Iowa Craft Beer Festival, and various biking events.
Seasonal/limited release beers: Inferno IPA, Smokey the Beer Porter, Smoked Molasses Grizzly Bear Stout, Burning Ember Black IPA, Walnut Brown, Honey Rhubarb, 3 Alarm Triple Red, and Double Smoked Stout.
Food: Snacks in house, rotating food trucks, local restaurant menus to order from.
Local non-beer attractions: The High Trestle Trail & Neal Smith Trail, Ankeny Market & Pavilion Park, Uptown Ankeny, Saylorville Lake, and Ankeny Farmer's Market.
Did you know? Dan smokes all his own malt for the smoked beers he produces.

Notes:

Franklin Street Brewing Company
Manchester

One of the youngest breweries in Iowa at press time was Manchester's Franklin Street Brewing Company (FSBC), owned by brothers Kyle and Chad Sands. After years of homebrewing and the occasional speculation of outfitting a brewery and shifting career paths, the Sands bore down in 2012 and began business planning their way to the historic Masonic Lodge building on Franklin Street. Built in 1875, the corner building that FSBC inhabits is across the street from the grocery store their grandfather, M.P. "Buck" Sands, owned. Though they grew up in Monticello, Kyle and Chad spent a fair amount of time in Manchester as kids, and their grandfather's business past served as an impetus for locating in Manchester. "We thought it would be neat to have another family business in the same town as Grandpa did," says Kyle.

In addition to the family angle, the Sands saw Manchester (and the specific building they chose) as an opportune location for a small brewery, being centrally situated among communities like Cedar Rapids, Waterloo, and Dubuque, among others. The Manchester Whitewater Park—a manmade whitewater course with six 18-inch drops over the course of the 800-foot course on the Maquoketa River—will be constructed within sight of the brewery's taproom (to be open by Spring of 2015), giving kayak enthusiasts a place to relax just a few steps from their playground.

Though the Masons still meet upstairs, the street-level brewery and taproom occupy a former hardware store. The Sands' building conversion added a five-barrel brewhouse to supply a gorgeous taproom which boasts original flooring, rustic brick walls, and exposed wood beams overhead. Kyle and Chad reclaimed and repurposed bricks and wood wherever possible. The result is a comfortable setting, whether one selects a table, the bar, or a couch to crash and share a beer with a friend.

Test batches hit the tanks in late March of 2014, and the Sands brothers conducted soft openings to work out the glitches, before closing the doors to fill their nine serving tanks with fresh beer for opening day. Moving forward, imbibers can expect a stout, brown ale, IPA, pale ale, blonde, hefeweizen, and a hoppy red ale in the early days as the Sands sift through local palate preferences before twisting in other directions, which most certainly will include a rhubarb beer to coincide with Manchester's annual Rhubarb Fest. And there's motivation to cycle in lagers down the road. "I'm a sucker for a Czech Pilsner," says Kyle, who intends to brew a beer in the meantime that he calls Big Frank. It's a Pils-inspired Moravian ale which is named for Kyle's brother-in-law, who lives in Czech Republic.

FSBC does not serve food, but carrying-in is fine, and the brothers intend to bring in food trucks and occasional caterers (as well as live music) so that sustenance is a possibility while sipping on tasty brews in Manchester's only brewery. Initially, on-site is the only place to track down the Franklin Street lineup, but as the dust settles, the Sands have plans to do small-scale packaging to reach a wider audience.

The Details

Franklin Street Brewing Company
116 South Franklin Street
Manchester, Iowa 52057
(319) 389-6873

Online: FranklinStreetBrewing.com, Facebook, Twitter
Owners: Kyle Sands and Chad Sands
Brewmaster: Kyle Sands
Year opened: 2014
Brewing system: 5-barrel
Tours: Yes
Availability: On-site by draught and growler
Parking: Street parking and public parking in lots across the street to the west and south
Year-round beers: Big Frank Moravian Ale (light Pilsner style, brewed with ale yeast), Milepost Pale Ale, Two Mile India Pale Ale, Burrington Brown Ale, Devil's Backbone Stout
Seasonal/limited release beers: "Left Turn Only" series of stronger beers, doubles, and imperials.
Food: None; however, FSBC maintains a stack of menus for area restaurants and encourages delivery to the taproom.
Local non-beer attractions: the Manchester Whitewater Park is right across the street
Tip: Like it lighter? Try Kyle's Moravian Ale, Big Frank.

Notes:

Front Street Brewery

Davenport

Not to sound melodramatic, but the descent into downtown Davenport is beautiful, building anticipation for the river views and the delectable brews in store. And Front Street does not disappoint. Opening in 1992, Front Street Brewery in Davenport is one of the oldest breweries in Iowa, and it's presented in the "classic" brewpub style, if there is such a thing; it's located in a charming building packed with woodwork and exposed brick walls, with historic photos speaking to the history of the area.

Sitting at the confluence of the Mississippi and Rock Rivers, and centrally located between Des Moines and Chicago, Davenport is the largest of the Quad Cities (which is actually five cities, not four: Davenport, Bettendorf, Rock Island, Moline, and East Moline). Well-stocked with German and Irish immigrants who brought their brewing talents from Europe, Davenport was a hub of beer until temperance battles dampened spirits. Davenport and Scott County offered little support to the teetotaler's movement, fighting Prohibitionist amendments at the state level. In 1884, Mayor Ernst Glausen stood opposed and a local ordinance allowed the sale of beverages such as Mum, Seafoam, Cordial, Hop Nectar, and Kentucky Bluegrass.

Today, Front Street Brewery sits with a view of the Mississippi River and has suffered the consequences of rising waters—their Raging River Ale commemorates the 1993 flood that invaded the brewery—but trudges forth with comforting atmosphere, good food and tasty beers.

In 2012, owner/brewer Steve Zuidema tripled Front Street's brewing capacity by moving all production to a new brewhouse a few blocks away in the city-owned Freight House Building, which operates on a "food hub" model featuring a farmers market as well as other locally-oriented food businesses. Beer fits perfectly, and the second location raises the brewery's exposure while providing a second taproom for Steve to expose imbibers to his wares.

On a recent visit to the original brewpub, I found a healthy lunch crowd, a friendly bartender and a family of eight beers. Steve brews with a delicate hand and somehow I, a stout-and-blood kind of guy, really found myself drawn to his light and drinkable Davenport Gold. He had two fruit beers pouring, one with cherries (oh, the aroma!) and another with apricots. They were soft and beautiful, for the drinker drawn to such libations.

As I sat in this historic building on the river, I thought back to Davenport's raucous early days of growth, and I would have been disappointed to learn of a boring past for this location. The brewpub's East River Road address did not let me down, as I learned from the name of the stout—Bucktown—that the neighborhood had a red light reputation a century ago.

Word is that the nightlife has settled down from those rowdier days, but it's a lot of fun in a less seedy way—and the beer is definitely back.

The Details

Front Street Brewery
208 E. River Drive (brewpub)
421 W. River Drive (tasting room)
Davenport, Iowa 52801
(563) 322-1569

Online: frontstreetbrew.com, Facebook
Owners: Steve Zuidema and Jennie Ash
Brewmaster: Steve Zuidema
Year opened: 1992
Brewing system: 15-barrel
Tours: No
Availability: On draught at the brewpub and taproom
Parking: Yes
Year-round beers: Davenport Gold, Cherry Ale, Hefe Weizen, Bucktown Stout, Vanilla Porter, Raging River Pale Ale, India Pale Ale.
Seasonal/limited release beers: Nut Brown Ale, Winter Warmer Ale, Double IPA, Apricot Wheat, Saison
Food: Bistro-style
Local non-beer attractions: Skybridge, Rhythm City Davenport Casino, Modern Woodmen Park, and Davenport Ferris Wheel
Tip: Want something on the lighter side? Try Front Street's Davenport Gold.

Notes:

Granite City Food and Brewery

Clive, Cedar Rapids, Ellsworth, and Davenport

"There's a lot of misunderstanding of the process," says Cory O'Neel, brewmaster at Granite City Food and Brewery. "The more people get an understanding of what we're doing, the more that misunderstanding can go away, and we can be respected more for what it is that we are doing."

What Cory and his colleagues at Granite City (GC) are doing is brewing beer. But they do it in a slightly different way. It's known as Fermentus Interruptus™, and it's unique enough that GC has patented the process. They start with malted barley. They mash, they vorlauf, they sparge, they lauter, and they boil the wort, just like any brewer would. They add hops during the boil. And then they cool that wort down. Just like any other brewer would. But then Cory presses pause—he interrupts the brewing process.

I visited Cory at the Granite City Worthouse in Ellsworth, which is where all the GC brewing takes place up to this point. The next move for GC is unique in the industry. They truck fresh, unfermented wort from one production facility to 30 locations in 13 states. The wort is pumped into 12.5-barrel fermenters at each restaurant, where a beer manager takes up where Cory left off. They pitch yeast, monitor fermentation, filter, condition, and serve the beer on-site. "The process is complete, it's whole, and it's valid," says Cory. "There are no corners cut."

He asked the same questions as many others when he heard about the GC brewing concept, but after becoming involved in the process and managing the lab, Cory has been won over to the production style's advantages. And he's the right guy for the job. Cory has brewed and consulted extensively everywhere from Colorado to Hong Kong for the last two decades, sometimes working for himself and sometimes working for others. The Des Moines-born brewer returned to his home state to work for GC in 2006, after the brewery had recognized their need for improved quality control. Cory's microbiology background suited the role, and a year after hiring on, he earned the brewmaster's position.

The results for GC are improved economies of scale, reduced capital investment and labor cost, and greater consistency of product. "There are a lot of other models of brewpub chains, and they are doing the same thing, but if they had 30 locations, they would have 30 brewhouses and 30 brewmasters and 30 water sources," says Cory. "We've just condensed that portion of it."

However, Cory notes that there are disadvantages to contend with: contamination of the product is at a greater risk. To combat the concern of infection, GC has a full analytical laboratory—one of the largest in Iowa—for testing and retesting of their yeast, wort and finished beer. It's tested at each stage of production, and when truck drivers deliver wort to the chain's stores, they pick up field samples to return to the lab for analysis. "I don't think a lot of people realize how tight we run the lab so that we can do the Fermentus Interruptus™ process," he says. "Because of what we do, there are so many more factors for contamination than a standard brewery would have. We have to be extra careful and vigilant with our microbiology. We have control over every part of the process. The lab is the heart of the whole operation as far as I'm concerned."

Working on a skeleton crew producing 20,000 barrels of beer per year, two brewers labor through 12-hour shifts to bang through five batches per day on a 25-barrel brewhouse. Targeting the outskirts of growing communities when selecting locations for their restaurants, GC, which has been called "the silent giant," focuses on brewing approachable beers to service a clientele that has perhaps never tasted craft beer before, building a loyal following as they educate their customers on what beer "should taste like and could taste like," says Cory. More recently, GC has delved into more assertive styles, offering a double IPA and Belgian strong ale to accommodate increasingly savvy palates.

In addition to its beer, GC produces all of their yeast in a 40-barrel propagator of the same scale as Wyeast and White Labs, two of the country's most notable suppliers of yeast for professional and homebrewers. While some beer enthusiasts might mistrust Fermentus Interruptus™, Cory's fellow professional brewers around the state trust him, his lab and GC's processes, as Cory quietly supplies yeast to a number of the breweries around the state.

Perfectly situated off I-35 to service their geographic footprint, the Worthouse quietly makes a lot of beer. For beer lovers looking for a beer and a good meal, there are three GC locations to visit in Iowa: Cedar Rapids, Clive, and Davenport.

The Details

Granite City Food & Brewery
Cedar Rapids
4755 1st Avenue SE
Cedar Rapids, Iowa 52403
(319) 395-7500

Granite City performs extensive labwork to ensure the quality of its product.

Clive
12801 University Avenue
Clive, Iowa 50325
(515) 224-1300

Davenport
5270 Utica Ridge Road
Davenport, Iowa 52807
(563) 344-970

Ellsworth (Worthouse)
1722 Detroit Street
Ellsworth, Iowa 50075
(515) 836-4060

Online: www.gcfb.net, Facebook, Twitter
Owner: Publicly traded corporation: Ticker symbol GCFB
Brewmaster: Cory O'Neel
Year opened: 1999
History of Company: First brewpub in St Cloud (The Granite City), second location Sioux Falls, SD. Built Production Brewery in Ellsworth Iowa in 2003. Currently 30 locations in 13 states.
Brewing system: 25-barrel brewhouse in Ellsworth; 12.5-15-barrel fermentation

capacity each brewpub location. Current annual production 22,000 BBL/year.

Tours: Yes

Availability: Draught and growlers available for purchase onsite.

Parking: Ample parking at all locations

Year-round beers: Northern Lager, Bennie Bock, The Duke Pale Ale, Batch 1000 DIPA, and Broad Axe Stout

Seasonal/limited release beers: Belgian Golden Strong Ale, Pride of Pilsen, Summer White Belgian Wit, Oak-Aged Scottish Ale, Oktoberfest, Burning Barn Irish Red Ale, Bluebarian Blueberry Lager, and Auntie Freeze Winter Warmer

Food: Scratch-made, American polished-casual

Did you know?: Granite City maintains an extensive lab to ensure quality control.

Notes:

Great River Brewery

Davenport

Nine hundred forty-one miles north of brewmaster/owner Paul Krutzfeldt's hometown of New Orleans, Great River Brewery in Davenport has served eastern Iowa's libation needs since 2009. Though relatively young, the Quad Cities production brewery is rooted in many years of evolution and a slow west-to-east migration that began when Paul served as the inaugural brewmaster at Rock Bottom in Des Moines when it opened in 1997.

After seven years at Rock Bottom, Paul and his partners bought the folding Fitzpatrick's Pub in Iowa City and, in 2004, started Old Capitol Brew Works, a brewpub utilizing kitchen staff that followed the popular brewmaster from Rock Bottom. Eventually, Paul's kitchen-side looked to step away from the brewpub, and rather than rewire a component of the project outside his skillset, Paul worked toward selling the building and setting up a production brewery. The brewhouse made the trek to Davenport in late 2008, and Paul's new Great River brand was up and running by February of 2009.

Housed within sight of the Mississippi River in a neighborhood that spent years in decay, Great River Brewery is one of many strengths of a downtown district on the mend. Previous incarnations of the locale included tire and muffler operations in a neighborhood comprised primarily of car dealerships and related businesses. Today, a 30-barrel brewhouse, backed by the state's first canning line, churns out a year-round family of beers including 483 Pale Ale, Roller Dam Red Ale, Farmer Brown Ale and Redband Stout, as well as a wide range of rotating seasonal beers.

I stopped by on the morning after a release party for one seasonal beer (Gingerbread Stout), and assistant brewer Kat Langford was hard at work brewing the next offering slated to replace it (Hopapotamus Double Dark Rye Pale Ale). While she tended to the brewhouse, co-owner Scott Lehnert and Trevor "T-Rev" Krutzfeldt manned the canning line, pushing out fresh 483. It's worth pointing out that if you've never had an 11 a.m. pale ale straight off the packaging line, you've not really lived.

Live I did during my tour, and Paul made sure my glass had something interesting in it all along the way. While there, I tried the aforementioned pale ale, as well as Big Cock IPA, a barrel-aged version of Farmer Brown and the Gingerbread Stout, an impy milk stout (clocking in at about 10% ABV) brewed with candied ginger, local honey, vanilla and a soft spice blend of cinnamon, nutmeg and clove. Yes, it was yummy.

And yummy equals strong sales, something that Great River has enjoyed straight out of the gates. On my visit, I found dated tanks marking an ongoing need to boost capacity, as well as a 14-tap tasting room expansion in the works. To increase space for onsite imbibers, Paul bought a long-vacant gas station across the street to utilize as office space, then knocked a hole in the wall to sprawl his bar area into his former pencil-pushing zone.

The expansion will offer a view of the canning line, which boasts a first on the planet for beer packaging: sleeved branding. "I was at a grocery store and started seeing all these sleeved products, and I was thinking, there's got to be somebody that does something like this for beer," says Paul. "It turns out there's not. So we looked into the investment that we'd have to put in for equipment for something that might not work for beer. We decided to do it like we usually do it and be the guinea pig."

The innovation helps Great River manage its 5,000 square feet of floor space more efficiently, and other breweries have taken notice. "Now we're getting calls to go to packaging expos and be guest speakers and other breweries come to visit us," Paul says.

Adapting the packaging strategy that had been used elsewhere in the beverage industry—juice and other soft drinks—has required some fine-tuning, but the Great River crew has made it work.

Always tweaking the beers, equipment and brewing protocols to improve the Great River products and their consistency, Paul has his eyes set on increasing his barrel-aging capacity and has been working with Mississippi River Distillery in nearby LeClaire to acquire space adjacent to the distillery for added capacity specifically geared toward seasonals and barrels—but there are obstacles to the project, and thirsty fans will have to wait to see how that plan plays out.

The Details

Great River Brewery
332 East 2nd Street
Davenport, Iowa 52801
(319) 541-5160

Online: greatriverbrewery.com, Facebook, Twitter
Owners: Paul Krutzfeldt, Scott and Dawn Lehnert, Pierce Eckhoff, and Lisa Woodring
BrewOps: Paul Krutzfeldt
Head Brewer: Scott Lehnert
Year opened: 2004
Brewing system: 30-barrel
Tours: Yes

Availability: Cans and draught in Iowa and Illinois
Parking: Street
Year-round beers: 483 Pale Ale, Roller Dam Red Ale, Farmer Brown Ale, and
    Redband Stout
Seasonal/limited release beers: Widespread Wit, Dark One IPA, Chicawawa
    Lemonale, Bix St. Copper Ale, Oktoberfest, Big Cock IPA, Dark Pumpkin,
    Imperial Gingerbread Stout, Golden Ale, Aaah! Bock, Christmas Beer, Herd West
    Coast IPA, Hopapotamus Double Dark Rye Pale Ale, Owney Irish Red Ale, Dos
    Pistolas, Barrel Aged Farmer, Arsenal Amber, and Dirty Blonde
Food: No, but you're welcome to bring your own or order in.
Did you know? Great River's Red Band Stout was named to Thrillis.com's list of
    the "Top 11 Stouts in the World." Give it a try!

Notes:

Brewer Paul Krutzfeldt
considers a recipe for an upcoming, limited-release beer.

Guerrilla Brewing Company
Waterloo

The coolest strip mall in America is in Waterloo, Iowa.

Barry Eastman owns Falls Mall, which houses not only Guerrilla Brewing Company (co-owned by Ty Graham, who doubles as head brewer), but also a pair of retro bars (Lava Lounge and The Beer Hall) and a full service Mexican restaurant (Rudy's Tacos). High school buddies and longtime fans of craft beer, Barry and Ty collaborated to bring Guerrilla Brewing Company to life in 2011. Concentrating on big beers (nothing less than 7 % ABV) in small batches (15 gallons a pop), the brewery is nestled into 700 square feet of space on a small strip mall of sorts located on the corner of Falls and Ansborough Avenues.

When I walked into the Lava Lounge, and then again at The Beer Hall, I felt I'd stepped into a time machine. Completely different in execution and vibe, both bars feel like about 1977 (or maybe 1981). For me, it felt like a Thursday night visit to Pee Wee's for a fish sandwich and cheeseballs and a couple games of Pac Man while listening to Joan Jett belt "I Love Rock 'n Roll" on the jukebox. But for Ty, these well thought out bars were more akin to the Circle Lounge or White House of his youth. "Those are the kinds of places that my dad would go on a Saturday with his buddy," Ty says of the vintage gems. "My mom would yell as he was leaving the house, 'Take Ty with you!' I'd go and play pool, and they'd have some beers."

And like GBC, both bars are a little bit guerrilla. "You would not know that this stuff is in here unless you know that this stuff is in here," says Ty.

Patrons can order in one bar and drink in another if they fancy a different décor. Or they can take their beer to Rudy's and order a taco. Customers and bartenders alike can be found running down offerings from the sister establishments housed under the same roof.

"It's a terrible business model," says Ty of the uber-small style favored by GBC. "But it is good if you want to make really good beers. Ours go on tap on Thursday (exclusively at The Beer Hall) and rarely make it to Saturday. You can only get it at one place at one time. It's not a business model for anyone who wants to make any money and get rich, but what we can do is, quite frankly, whatever the fuck we want to do. There's so much to be said for that."

That he does. Try a 10.3% juniper brown ale on for size. Or an 11% chocolate-covered bacon stout. Or a 13.5% ginger ale, a golden beer with a ginger punch that Ty recommends as the base for a Mexican Mule, a tequila-based takeoff on the Moscow Mule. "Ninety to ninety-five percent of everything that we do is imperial—and something turned on its ear," said Ty, who brews "hybrids of hybrids," as well as the occasional "straight-up IPA." "We go in different directions all the time," he says.

A pending black IPA called Two Hops For Sure, a Tupac Shakur-tribute beer (as well as a bourbon barrel-aged version), calls attention to the influence of music in Ty's brewhouse. On a recent kite surfing trip to Cabo San Lucas, Ty conceived a beer called Mexican Blackbird, which takes its inspiration from the ZZ Top song of the same name. Without a doubt, it will be big, small, interesting and guerrilla.

Staying small—staying guerrilla—doesn't mean that Ty has no plans to grow. That may happen. In the meantime, Ty focuses on GBC's mission statement: To make the next batch of beer the best one that we have ever made. "Sometimes we hit it, and sometimes we don't," he says. "But it's always really close."

Because size doesn't matter, everyone should know about what's happening at 2401 Falls Avenue. While I'd heard of it early on, I'd never tasted the beers or talked with Ty until el Bait Shop's Little Giant Beer Summit in October of 2013. It was a memorable moment, because he was branding beer. I don't mean to say he was conceptualizing a label, story and Tweet campaign. I mean he had submerged a red hot poker into a goblet of beer to caramelize the residual sugars in the cherry impy stout he had on offer. "I do that when the mood strikes me or when I'm celebrating something specific," he says.

Something specific might be his birthday or a Thursday afternoon. You never know. And turning to a website will offer the everyday beer drinker little help. Ty has heretofore stuck to Facebook to alert fans to what he's up to. "Being guerrilla, we're really covert about it. Not that I'm a technophobe or an anti-technology guy," says the professional firefighter. "But I do have another job and a couple other businesses, so maintaining a Facebook site is easier for us."

So click "like" and pay attention on Thursdays. That's the only way to know what's happening at this covert nano operation.

The Details

Guerrilla Brewing Company
2401 Falls Avenue
Waterloo, Iowa 50701

Online: Facebook
Owners: Ty Graham and Barry Eastman
Brewmaster: Ty Graham
Year opened: 2011
Brewing system: ½-barrel
Tour info: Yes
Availability: On draught, only at The Beer Hall
Parking: Parking lot
Year-round beers: It doesn't work like that here
Seasonal/limited release beers: All of them
Food: Mexican-American food at Rudy's Tacos
Tip: Follow Guerrilla Brewing on Facebook—it's the only way to know what Ty's up to.

Notes:

Iowa River Brewing Company

Marshalltown

I'll admit that I questioned my GPS when it told me I'd arrived. It was dark, and I strained my eyes, but I couldn't see it. I'd driven too far to give up, and thank goodness I'd investigated Iowa River Brewing Company's website before departing; the logo was fresh in my mind, and I thought I could make it out in the moonlight reflecting off the snow. The GPS was right. Set back off the street and with an unlit sign, here it was.

Inside, I found a beautiful taproom that featured a cedar bar made from a century-old telephone pole and barn boards rescued from owner Roger Brown's family acreage. The character didn't stop there. Handmade tables, a restored wooden canoe, an antique cider press. It was a beautiful setting to share a pint, and the bustling crowd I walked into seemed to agree.

Always experimenting with different grains and yeast strains, Roger offers a wide assortment of beers on 13 taps. Functioning on a nimble, 50-gallon brewhouse, one of the aims of IRBC is selection. In his first year of business, Roger produced 186 different beers. On my visit, Roger was pouring a smoked wee heavy, a sweet Belgian, a witbier, a coffee beer, a hefeweizen, an oatmeal stout, a caramel beer, a rauchbier, an Amarillo pale ale, an IPA, a chocolate porter, and an Irish red ale. Of this gamut, only a couple represented recipes that had been repeated. I did my best to hit all on offer during my sojourn, and could see why patrons had requested a return of the Churchill Chocolate Porter.

Adding to the variety of Roger's brewing toils is the offer of "private label" brewing, which is to say that IRBC will craft a custom beer for weddings, birthdays, retirements, and other special occasions. Why serve Craft Beer X at your wedding reception when you can serve a one-off keg of Mr. and Mrs. X Ale? This is an idea that is sure to catch on.

Locals interested in an office party will surely jump all over IRBC's taproom, as its atmosphere and private label service should provide an enticing lure for groups under forty in number. It's a taproom only, so no food is served, but patrons are encouraged to bring in food from other sources, or to order in.

Located in the central part of the state, Marshalltown's Iowa River Brewing Company provides wide variety in a charming setting, and is worth the trip.

The Details

Iowa River Brewing Company
107 North First Street
Marshalltown, Iowa 50158
(641) 753-1140

Online: iowariverbrewing.com, Facebook
Owners: Roger and Ellen Brown
Brewmaster: Roger Brown
Year opened: 2013
Brewing system: 3-barrel
Tours: No
Availability: Draught and growlers onsite
Parking: Parking lot
Year-round beers: Heavy rotation is the name of the game here.
Annual event: Oktoberfest (late-September)
Seasonal/limited release beers: Heavy rotation is the name of the game here.
Food: No, but carry-ins are welcome.
Local non-beer attractions: Marshall County Historical Museum, Matchstick Marvels, GrimesFarm & Conservation Center, Glick-Sower Heritage Homestead, Matthew Edel Blacksmith Shop, Meskwaki Bingo-Casino, and Orpheum Theater Center
Tip: Who knows if they'll brew it again, but I loved the Rausch Star, a deliciously bacony smoked beer.

Notes:

Jubeck New World Brewing Company

Dubuque

Though the idea for Jubeck New World Brewing had fermented for years, making the dream a reality began in early 2013 when Jubeck Brewing won a $250 second prize in a community arts fundraising program called Art Gumbo. The money went toward purchasing stainless steel, which co-owner Jay Jubeck converted into a mash tun. Along with co-owner Dan Caraway, Jay then launched a successful Kickstarter (online crowd-funding platform) campaign, which brought in over $37,000 in startup capital for a unique business model designed to bring good beer back to Dubuque, an eastern Iowa city with a rich brewing history—but no breweries in the past few years.

Reversing the local beer drought, Jubeck New World Brewing set up as a Community Supported Brewery (CSB) fashioned after the premise of Community Supported Agriculture, in which individuals pledge financial support to a farm in exchange for the farm's bounty later in the growing season. JNWB offers locals the same membership program, though instead of zucchinis and tomatoes, members receive growlers of beer.

Though the concept isn't brand-new (House of Brews in Madison, Wisconsin and Begyle Brewing Company in Chicago, Illinois are two examples of breweries operating CSBs) the Kickstarter model offered creative financing to get the project off the ground. "It was an avenue for selling memberships in the CSB," says Jay. "It's essentially pre-sales—we have to deliver on the beer."

Jay and Dan acquired space at 115 West 11th Street in Dubuque in August of 2013, gutted it, and brought its exposed brick and punched-tin ceiling base layer back. Made from reclaimed yellow pine from one of Dubuque's old warehouses, the bar and tables in the taproom were custom made by a friend. Add to this atmosphere a lineup of small-batch beers and the growing craft beer community in Dubuque has a welcome new home for socializing.

Crediting the local homebrew shop, Bluff Street Brew Haus, for developing their own passion for brewing, Jay and Dan installed their 1.6-barrel (50 gallon) brewing system to produce the likes of their Lavender Honey Wheat, Apricot Pale Ale, Dark IPA, Warrior Stout, and Golden Hybrid Beer. JNWB offers three levels of membership to the CSB—full, half, and social—depending on how thirsty you are, but drop-in drinkers are welcome as well, and this place, replete with character, is worth a stop if you're passing through the Dubuque area.

The Details

Jubeck New World Brewing Company
115 West 11ᵗʰ Street
Dubuque, Iowa 52001
(563) 599-9242

Online: jubeckbrewing.com, Facebook
Owners: Jay Jubeck and Dan Caraway
Brewmaster: Jay Jubeck
Year opened: 2013
Brewing System: 1.6-barrel (50 gal.)
Tours: Yes
Availability: Draught in the taproom
Parking: Street parking, nearby parking ramp
Public Transportation: The Jule
Year-Round Beers: TBD
Seasonal/Limited Release Beers: TBD
Food: No, but deliveries are welcome.
Local Non-Beer Attractions: National Mississippi River Museum and Aquarium, Fenelon Place Elevator, Mines of Spain Recreation Area, Dubuque Arboretum and Botanical Gardens, Eagle Point Park, Mystique Ice Center, Bell Tower Theater, Diamond Jo Casino, Grand Harbor Resort and Waterpark, Sundown Mountain (skiing), Matter Creative Center, Dubuque Museum of Art, and Voices from the Warehouse Art Gallery.
Did you know? Jay and Dave became friends while playing in a band called The Fast Clydes.

Notes:

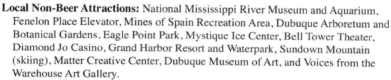

Kalona Brewing Company

Kalona

Oftentimes, beers reflect the personality of their creators, and that was undoubtedly the case when I paid a visit to Kalona Brewing Company (KBC). I tasted the judicious hand of Brewmaster Lew Brewer's complete line of beers that, to me, really echoed the kind-hearted, soft elements of Lew's personality. He laughed when I paid him this compliment, but admits: "We like flavor, and we like balance."

Without question, Lew's beers resemble this remark.

Lew started homebrewing thirty years ago, but his decision to open a brewery didn't come without professional experience. His first exposure to the commercial side of beer was working on the packaging line at Redhook Brewery in his native Seattle, Washington. Later, he brewed for Hale's Ales. "I couldn't afford to eat on what they paid me, so I went back to painting," he says.

His homebrewing persisted, and eventually Lew migrated to the Iowa City. There, he brewed for a time at Fitzpatrick's (closed 2004), and his idea for his own place continued to ferment in his mind. "The desire and the passion was still there, but it just wasn't happening." In September of 2012, Lew and co-owner Ted Nagy bought a corner building in Kalona, about 20 minutes south of I-80 and a 30 minutes' drive from Iowa City, and started the process of making his decades-old vision a reality.

The original plan was to be a production brewery with a taproom, but the City of Kalona didn't have zoning for this concept in the location they had purchased. It blew up their budget, but they added a full-service restaurant to make it work, and a brewpub was born. It's beautiful. If someone kidnapped you, drove you for three hours, and brought you to KBC, you'd walk in, freshly unblindfolded, and swear you were in a big city.

Rustic elements like polished cement floors, cinderblock walls and a barn board dropped ceiling over the bar are juxtaposed next to exposed steel I-beams, a leather sofa seating area, and big glass revealing a view of the stainless jungle that is Lew's 15-barrel brewhouse. Large-format black and white historical photos peek at the past, while 26 tap handles on the wall peek to the future.

KBC opened in September of 2013, and Lew has drawn a thirsty audience from miles around, both those imbibing onsite at the taproom and those purchasing the 32-ounce growlettes he distributes to a number of off-premise accounts. Starting with his Lew-bricator, a wheat doppelbock, and his Sucha Much IPA, Lew will have cans in stores sometime in the late Spring of 2014. "We might have to get a couple more tanks [to keep up]," says a smiling Lew, pleased with the reaction from consumers.

Lew serves a wide range of beer styles, from a light lager to an imperial stout, complemented by the likes of Vienna lager, English mild, black IPA and as many as three interpretations of saison flowing at a time. And there's always something new. I was lucky enough to try Lew's first big batch of Golden Glow Pale Ale straight from the tank. "I've been brewing Golden Glow for thirty years, and have never been satisfied, until this," he says. "I tweaked it, did a pilot batch and that turned out very nice, so I went ahead and did a big batch."

Dry-hopped with Centennial and Amarillo hops, Lew had settled in on a fine pale ale that patrons will most certainly enjoy. They will enjoy the atmosphere of the restaurant, they will enjoy the beers, and they'll drink Lew into a little more work to do. Which is a welcome and rewarding thank-you after so many years of planning.

The Details

Kalona Brewing Company
405 B Avenue
Kalona, Iowa 52247
(319) 656-3335

Online: kalonabrewing.com, Facebook
Owners: Ted Nagy and Lew Brewer
Brewmaster: Lew Brewer
Opened: 2013
Brewing system: 15-barrel
Availability: draught in Kalona, Iowa City, Washington,
   and Oxford; cans on the horizon
Parking: Yes
Year-round beers: Sucha Much IPA, Kalona Classic, Double Whammy Imperial
   Stout, Mild Start English Session Brown, Quick Wit, Say What? Saison, Vienna
   Symphony, Black to the Future Black IPA
Seasonal/limited release beers: Oktoberfest, Lewbricator, You Be You Imperial Stout
Food: Wood-fired pizzas and more
Did you know?: Kalona Brewmaster Lew Brewer cut his teeth in the brewing
   industry at Red Hook and Hale's Ales in Seattle.

Notes:

Keg Creek Brewing Company

Glenwood

Keg Creek Brewing Company once gave me a warm fuzzy. Of all the breweries in the state, at one hour's drive, KCBC is the closest brewery to my rural southwest Iowa front door. On one sunny afternoon, it stood between me and an appointment in Omaha, Nebraska. So, of course, I stopped in for a beer. Since their opening in 2011, I've become well-acquainted with the trio of homebrewers-turned-brewery owners, Randy Romens, Art Renze and John Bueltel (as well as Grant Hebel, who helped get the brewery open and has since moved on). The Keg Creek beers are, as is the case with so many breweries, a reflection of the brewers behind them. In this case, that means the beers are kind, gentle, laid-back and good-hearted. Keg Creek offers easy-drinking, to-style versions of the beers they produce.

Pulled into the business by a community that adored their homebrew, the Keg Creek guys brew on a three-barrel system a couple of blocks from Glenwood's downtown square in what had once been a gas station and, later, a pizza place. They pulled together a transformation of the space to offer a clean and inviting taproom, as well as an outside beer garden, from which to push out their family of beers with names tied to their local community.

Keg Creek Brewing Company (and its IPA) is, for starters, named for a nearby stream, which was once called Five Barrel Creek after a cache of whisky was discovered by the United States Dragoons. An 1843 map on the foyer wall at the brewery shows the creek with its original name telling the tale of this contraband trade with local Native Americans in what is now the Glenwood area. Other local monikers are attached to beers such as Wabash Wheat, Wayesa Cream Ale, and Sharp Street Stout. Stop by the tap room for drinkable beers, friendly conversation and an occasional epiphany.

To date, they haven't thrown down a Double IPA. They haven't brewed a Russian Imperial Stout. They haven't used bugs, bacon or brownie mix in any of their beers. Their beers are loving grandpas, lifelong friends, supportive uncles.

John, who heads up the brewing duties, was behind the bar the day of a mind-opening visit I shan't soon forget. As always, his beers were delicious, and it was a pity that I was on a short timetable. I had time for one beer and one sample (a saison and a maltzbier, respectively, as I recall). There were a handful of locals chatting at the bar somewhere in the four o'clock hour. John and I caught up, and I enjoyed getting to know a few of the good folks of Glenwood that day. I finished my beers, my train of thought and looked at the clock: time to go. Darn.

I bade John and the crew farewell, and took my leave. I walked out the door, and I kid you not, I felt just a little choked up by an inexplicable warm fuzzy, the likes of which can only be outdone by the love of a small child. I pondered this emotional outburst as I eased on down the road, and I decided that what felt so good in that brief moment was one of the great characteristics of beer: community. Beer brings people together; this we know. In this situation, my delight was a little bit of John, a retired art teacher; a little of his simple, yet well-executed, beers; and a little of the fact that I was having this good beer with this nice guy in a small town in Iowa. If I can get a good beer here, then I can most assuredly get a good beer anywhere in the world. What I felt as I left the brewery that day was gratitude, a deep sensation of thankfulness for both friendly folk and the ability to procure a beer of character in a place that was not long ago entirely awash in cheap, insipid straw-colored boredom.

What a delight that is!

I don't suppose that I'll be rewarded with the same epiphany on my next visit, but when I return, I can rest assured that John, Randy and Art will serve me up a pint of beer that reminds me of all my good uncles. Art will keep the pretzel bowl full, John will make me feel like the center of the universe, and Randy will show me new pictures of his grandkids. In short, they'll make me feel welcome while they live the dream carving out the next stage of their lives.

The Details

Keg Creek Brewing Company
111 Sharp Street
Glenwood, Iowa 51534
(712) 520-9029

Online: kegcreekbrewing.com and Facebook
Owners: Art Renze, John Bueltel, and Randy Romens
Brewmaster: John Bueltel
Year opened: 2011
Brewing system: 3-barrel
Tours: Yes
Availability: Glenwood, Omaha, Council Bluffs, Adel, and Des Moines. Packaging and selling 22-ounce bottles in Hy-Vees in Des Moines and Council Bluffs.
Parking: Lot
Public Transportation: No
Year-round beers: Wabash Wheat, Brick Red Ale, Waseya Cream Ale, Sharp Street Stout, Breakdown Brown, and Keg Creek IPA
Seasonal/limited release beers: Impure Thoughts Saison, Munich Helles, Black IPA, Black Lager, Apricot Wheat, Nitro Stout, Scottish Ale, and Malzbier

Annual events: Glenwood Homecoming, Keg Creek Days, Relay for
  Life Fundraisers

Local non-beer attractions: Mills County Historical Museum, Pony Creek Trail,
  Davies Amphitheater, Indian Earth Lodge, Glenwood Lake Park, and
  several wineries

Tip: You can't go wrong ordering a beer at Keg Creek. Each of their beers
  is a solid representation of its style.

*John Bueltel heads up the brewing duties at Glenwood's Keg Creek
Brewing Company.*

Notes:

Lake Time Brewery

Clear Lake

After moving twice within a 10-month span, and then having his surgical sales position eliminated, brewer Bob Rolling decided to ditch the rat race and head for the lake. Working to appreciate the simpler things in life, Bob created both a literal and figurative "lake time."

Lake Time Brewery is located in an early-1900s house just four blocks from Clear Lake, which is known for not only its summer recreational opportunities, but also for being the location of "The Day the Music Died"—the location where the airplane carrying rock and roll legends Buddy Holly, Ritchie Valens and J.P. "The Big Bopper" Richardson crashed, killing them all in the winter of 1959.

Looking to downshift, Bob converted a realtor's office, conference room, and reception area (the location had also been a funeral home in an earlier era) into a quaint and comfortable drinking environment unlike any other taproom in the state. Numerous windows pull in natural light year-round, and a working fireplace is the centerpiece to the prime drinking seats in the winter months. While locals have exceeded expectations with strong support during the winter months, the vacationers tend to swell the numbers in the summer, and Bob is working to expand his outdoor seating to accommodate anticipated crowds.

With beach-driven interior decorating handled by Bob's wife, Suzy, the deeper element of conversion took place in the brewery area. Bob started with a 15-gallon system when he opened in June of 2013, but scaled up to a 1-barrel brewhouse in February of 2014 to ease his brewing schedule. While the move doubled his output, with 10 beers on tap (eight regulars, including a gluten-reduced ale, and two seasonal offerings) and many happy patrons, Bob still brews frequently to stay fully stocked in beer.

Bob's Sandy Bottoms American Wheat has been his best seller, followed by his Rusty Rudder Brown Ale, though his 9.1% ABV Anchors Away Imperial Stout was his number two seller for a surprisingly long time, according to Bob. In keeping with his lake-themed beer names, Bob calls his IPA "Propeller," which also alludes to his practice of constantly toying with the recipe. In addition to lake names, beers occasionally recall that famous crash—I fancied the Peggy Sue Pub Ale on my visit, and Bob had a Sock Hop Pale Ale in the works.

Homey atmosphere seems a trite descriptor for a taproom that is itself a converted home, but that's what it is. Service and atmosphere are important to Bob, and are sometimes intangible parts of enjoying a beer. Lake Time's attention to this detail makes for a good-feeling place to drink beer.

The Details

Lake Time Brewery
801 Main Avenue, Suite C
Clear Lake, Iowa 50428
(641) 357-2040

Online: laketimebrewery.com, Facebook and Twitter
Owners: Bob and Suzy Rolling
Brewmaster: Bob Rolling
Year opened: 2013
Brewing system: 1-barrel
Tours: Yes
Availability: taproom only
Parking: Public, private and street parking
Public Transportation: yes
Year-round beers: American Wheat, Pale Ale, IPA, Amber Ale, Brown Ale, Porter, Imperial Stout on Nitro, and Gluten Reduced Ale
Seasonal/limited release beers: Coffee Brown Ale, Raspberry Cream Ale, Brown Porter, SMaSH series, Harvest Ale, Pumpkin Spice Ale, and more…
Food: Meat and Cheese trays available
Local non-beer attractions: Clear Lake is known for its summer attractions and very active chamber of commerce. Local attractions include the historic Surf Ballroom, Clear Lake Arts Center, and Central Gardens of North Iowa. Visit the memorial at the plane crash site of Buddy Holly, Ritchie Valens, and J.P. "The Big Bopper" Richardson, where the plane came to rest following their final concert at the Surf Ballroom in 1959. Enjoy the lake on one of Clear Lake's beaches, at the state park, boating, fishing, swimming, or sailing. Take a ride on The Lady of the Lake. Activities include the Winter Dance Party, which marks the anniversary of the day the music died; Color the Wind Kite Festival; Bicycle Blues and BBQ; Iowa Storytelling Festival; a weeklong 4th of July celebration; CLASS Car Show and Summer Dance Cruise; Fall Harvest Festival, and Christmas by the Lake.
Tip: Located in an early-1900s-era house, Lake Time Brewery's taproom is cozy and truly unique—a must-see in the state and only a few blocks from the lake.

Notes:

Lion Bridge Brewing Company

Cedar Rapids

Lion Bridge Brewing Company is named after the Bridge of Lions, which connects the Czech Village in which it is situated and the New Bohemia District (NewBo). Owner/Brewmaster Quinton McClain has 50 percent Czech ancestry, but points out that LBBC is not necessarily a "Czech-style brewery." Mindful of the Czech heritage of its locale, LBBC is a small brewery that appreciates and hopes to contribute to "the sense of community in this charming neighborhood."

Years in the making and opening to the public beginning in March of 2014, LBBC marks Quinton's return to his native Cedar Rapids after time teaching and writing in Argentina and brewing in Fort Collins, Colorado. The former brewer at Fort Collins Brewing Company gained valuable professional experience there, making beer, doing sales and promotions, working on the bottling line, driving a delivery truck and everything in between. "It's important to learn the best way to scrub a keg and the best way to hose down a floor—and take pride in it," he says of the elements of a brewer's life about which most people are unaware.

Quinton installed his 10-barrel brewhouse in the former Fritz's Food Market, which opened in the 1930s. More recently, the 7,000-square-foot building sat empty until the National Czech and Slovak Museum and Library (NCSML) purchased it in 2012 to avoid demolition. Though there are Swiss cheese elements to the neighborhood as a result of severe flooding in 2008, the area is making a comeback, and Quinton is pleased to be a part of the resurgence of artisan producers breathing new life into the historic locale.

The NCSML and the Bridge of Lions itself are but a stone's throw away, along with a number of bars, a bakery and a sausage maker (which uses Quinton's beer in some of their sausages). The area is packed with character, as is LBBC.

After a long life as a supermarket, the building housing the brewery itself is less Old World in style than some of its surroundings, but Quinton has created a modern-vibed space that showcases not only his beers but also his brewhouse behind glass, a copper bar and industrial elements that make for a suitable drinking niche for today's beer lover.

As for his launching beers, Quinton's Ziva Voda (pronounced sheeva voda) was the lone Czech-leaning style. Translated into English, the moniker means "living water," a beautiful sentiment indeed. It presents "like a Pilsner," though it ferments with a German ale yeast rather than the lager yeast used for the production of a true Pilsner. Quinton also offered a smoked chocolate stout, an English dark mild, a Belgian wheat ale, and a Belgian IPA. Quinton takes his influence from all over the globe, and he intends to put out a variety of beers and allow the public to help shape the brewery's lineup.

With an appreciation for the past as well as the future of American beer, Quinton has succeeded in bringing new life to an old part of a town. Quinton's living water is but one piece of the puzzle, but what a beautiful picture it is that his vision is helping to create.

Lion Bridge brewer Quiton McClain offers a sample at his Cedar Rapids brewery.

The Details

Lion Bridge Brewing Company
59 16th Avenue SW
Cedar Rapids, Iowa 52404
(319) 200-4460

Online: lionbridgebrewing.com, Facebook, Twitter, and Instagram
Owners: Quinton McClain and Deborah Kaiser
Brewmaster: Quinton McClain
Year opened: 2014
Brewing system: 10-barrel
Tours: Yes
Availability: Available on draught in the Lion Bridge Pub and at select accounts in Eastern Iowa; growler purchases at the brewery.
Parking: Approximately 20 spots for Lion Bridge Brewing Company and seven acres of free parking located in the Czech Village.
Public Transportation: Cedar Rapids City Bus
Year-round beers: Undetermined at press time. Year-round beers will develop organically based on brewer preference and patron feedback.
Seasonal/limited release beers: Undetermined
Food: A small menu of beercentric foods that changes seasonally and utilizes local farmers and artisans as much as possible.
Local non-beer attractions: Czech and Slovak Museum and Library, Cedar Rapids Museum of Art, Cedar Rapids Public Library, NewBo City Market, Paramount Theatre, Theatre Cedar Rapids, Brucemore, Cedar Valley Bike Trail, Downtown Farmer's Market (summer only), Czech Village, New Bohemia District, The Cherry Building, The Ceramics Center, The Amana Colonies, US Cellular Center, Grant Wood Studio, and Prairiewoods Franciscan Spirituality Center
Did you know? Quinton's mom is an artist, and she designed the Lion Bridge logo, which hearken to the cement lions adorning the bridge after which the brewery is named.

Notes:

Lost Duck Brewing Company
Fort Madison

The most southeastern brewery in the state, Lost Duck Brewing Company, is housed in a building (two buildings, actually) that was constructed in 1864 by the railroad to cater to worker morale (nudge, nudge). Perched on the banks of the Mighty Mississippi, the gambling house and brothel would later serve as a doctor's office, apartment building and barbershop before Dr. Tim Benson, a Fort Madison chiropractor, would give himself a part-time job in the late 1990s by converting the space one more time into its current function: a brewpub.

Located in one of the few places where the Mississippi River runs east to west rather than north to south, Lost Duck takes its name from the confused-looking migrating waterfowl who seem to engage in an above-average amount of time circling overhead as if trying to get their bearings straight. On a 3.5-barrel brewing system, Tim makes a different kind of magic in the upstairs of the restored property, offering a wide range of ales and lagers to thirsty patrons.

On my visit, I circled 10 offerings: a light lager, American wheat, Pilsner, White IPA, honey lager, pale ale, Belgian dubbel, red ale and a porter. For the kids, Tim offers a pair of house-brewed sodas: root beer and cream soda. The kitchen keeps it local, as well, serving locally-sourced bison, elk, and bratwurst.

The atmosphere is clean and fresh, with rustic brick walls, attractive woodwork, and glassware drawing in the sunshine from the 12-foot tall, east-facing plate glass windows looking out on the railroad, the river, a replica of the original Fort Madison, and the Illinois shore across the river. There are no televisions on the walls, which encourages conversation. On my visit, a knot of regulars discussed homegrown chili peppers, salsas, and the Scoville scale, and as something of a salsa geek, it was a refreshing discourse in a beautiful setting.

I was the only non-local in the establishment that Friday afternoon, but I was made to feel welcome by hot conversation with my new comrades, who were as refreshing as a cold lager on a hot day. I walked in a lost duck, but thanks to the barley alliance I'd forged while sitting at the bar, I did not leave one.

The Details

Lost Duck Brewing Company
723-725 Avenue H (Highway 61)
Fort Madison, Iowa 52627
(319) 372-8255

Soaked in beer history, Fort Madison Lost Duck Brewing Company is housed in a former gambling house and brothel.

Online: duckbrewing.com, Facebook

Owner/Brewmaster: Dr. Tim Benson

Year opened: 2003

Brewing system: 3.5-barrel

Tours: Yes

Availability: Draught onsite, growlers/kegs

Parking: Lot

Year-round beers: American Wheat, Pintail Pale Ale, Ringneck Red Lager, Pelican Porter, Premium Pilsner

Seasonal/limited release beers: Brewer's whim

Food: Pub-style

Local non-beer attractions: Mississippi River

Did you know?: The building that houses Lost Duck Brewing Company was built by the railroad in 1864.

Notes:

Madhouse Brewing Company

Des Moines

Transition. It's a word that describes much of the craft brewing industry not only across the country but also within Iowa. Many breweries are expanding capacity, adding packaging lines, and augmenting their businesses in a variety of ways. For Madhouse Brewing Company, which opened in Newton in 2009, change includes not only adding space and a tasting room, but moving all production to Des Moines.

With retail/taproom limitations on the ground in Newton, the entire Madhouse staff residing in Des Moines, and Brewmaster Mason Groben's family owning a building on Scott Avenue in the Lower East Village, the geographical shift made sense. I visited the new brewery in early March of 2014 and found something that looked a lot more like a construction zone. Mason walked me through the plans, an ambitious shift that will be good for not only the business, but for Iowa beer drinkers.

A year in planning, the project was proceeding in stages. Commencing brewing operations was the number one goal to replenish Madhouse's accounts and satiate the thirsts of eager fans. With one-third more space than they had in their previous location and a new taproom, the move would also allow Madhouse to increase production and situate themselves with a retail dimension in the midst of a larger market, while ramping up the brewery's barrel program. While the brewhouse (and paperwork) was in place on the day of my visit, a round of cleaning stood in the way before the brewery was wort-ready. But Mason has been through moves of this kind before. His parents, Jean and Paul Groben, own Jasper Winery, which also migrated from Newton to Des Moines.

With a 2003 degree in viticulture and enology from UC-Davis, Mason started on the wine-side with his parents, and then helped launch Madhouse in 2009, when the tireless fermenter discovered the seasonality of wine production left him with time on his hands in the winter months. And so Mason heads up production at both Jasper and Madhouse. "We've taken a different route. Up until now, we were production only," he says. But with brands developed and the itch to increase barreled offerings as well as to have a tasting room to better serve customers, the time has come for Madhouse to shift and grow.

While Madhouse has dabbled in barrel-aged beers, Mason looks to increase production of these beers, and part of this ambition includes a new line of sour beers. He's currently developing recipes for this facet of the plan, which will likely begin with a sour saison brewed with a French saison yeast. A kriek and a dark sour are both on the agenda, and all of Mason's sours will see time in the barrel. This dream is a sure reality, as there were 20 fresh Jack Daniels whiskey barrels just waiting to be filled when I stopped by. "The first time you use the barrel, it's going to be extracting the whisky or whatever was in it," Mason explained. "After that, it's a lot more neutral barrel, which is going to be best used for making sour beer—we won't be looking to get as much extraction of the whisky, but more to get a little of the oak and the microbes that affect the beer, and the barrels will harbor the microorganisms that are going to sour the beer."

So beers will go in, and beers will go out. And then the sour line will find its starting point. As Madhouse has demonstrated, the starting line moves around from time to time. They started in Newton, and now they start again in Des Moines. The latter is the beginning of a wonderful new beginning, one that ushers in more space and more beers. What a good start for the East Village beer scene!

The Details

Madhouse Brewing Company
501 Scott Avenue
Des Moines, Iowa 50309

Online: madhousebeer.com, Facebook, Twitter
Owners: Over 20 investors
Brewmaster: Mason Groben
Year opened: 2009
Brewing system: 15-barrel
Tours: Yes
Parking: Yes
Public Transportation: Yes
Availability: 12- and 22-ounce bottles, draught
Year-round Beers: Honey Pilsner, Pastime Pale Ale, Hopburst IPA, Oak-aged Imperial Red, and Coffee Stout
Tip: I'm a fan of Madhouse's Coffee Stout—give it a try!

Notes:

Maple City Brewing Company
Osage

Owned by Pat and Kate Kealiher, Maple City is a tiny, production-only nanobrewery located next to Taste. (By Unc's Cheesecakes) and Cabin Coffee Company in Osage. As I eyed the small, one-barrel brewing system located in a galley about as wide as my wingspan, I couldn't help but dream of knocking a hole in the wall to meld the three concepts. What could be better than cheesecake, coffee, and beer? I smell a collaboration.

Kate snapped me back to reality as she showed me around, and noted that eventually, they'd be installing a taproom in the back section of the building. In the meantime, the Maple City beers, are only available on draught in a handful of local restaurants and bars. Maple City Brewing Company is small, and the brewery isn't really set up for a visit, but there are plans for growth. During my visit, Pat was planning a transition to dedicate himself to the brewery on a fulltime basis, and working toward an online crowd funding campaign to build capital. Shifting fulltime to Maple City will allow more time for brewing, spreading the good word, and working toward that taproom.

So keep your eyes peeled for Sage Hopper IPA and Kealiher Irish Red. Pat has more beer on the way.

The Details

Notes:

Maple City Brewing Company
518 Main Street
Osage, Iowa 50461
(641) 832-0278

Online: Facebook
Owners: Pat and Kate Kealiher
Brewmaster: Pat Kealiher
Year opened: 2012
Brewing system size/capacity: one-barrel
Hours: Wholesale only. No open hours
Tours: Call or message on Facebook
Availability: On tap at northern Iowa bars and restaurants.
Parking: Street
Public Transportation: No
Year-round beers: Sage Hopper IPA, Kealiher's Irish Red
Local non-beer attractions: Spring Park
Tip: Maple City's IPA and Irish Red are only available in northern Iowa.

Mason City Brewing Company

Mason City

A trio of homebrewers who had an avid fan base within their circle of friends, Arian Schuessler, Jake Rajewsky, and Justin Merritt eventually decided to look into the notion of opening a brewery after the "you should sell this" comments piled up.

In the spring of 2012, they launched a Kickstarter campaign to help raise funds for the venture. The brewers established a $15,000 goal, and when the dust settled, they'd raised $23,500 on the online crowdsourcing platform. "That showed us that the community was definitely ready and willing to support us," says Jake.

The building the brewers procured wasn't on the market, but they saw the underutilized auxiliary space attached to an interior designer's storefront. They approached the designer about moving into the location, and Mason City Brewing Company (MCBC) was on its way to becoming a reality. MCBC opened its doors in February of 2013, and at the time, all three partners in the venture intended to keep their day jobs while growing their business. But a month after launching, Jake left his job as a photographer for the Mason City Globe-Gazette to keep the brewhouse under control. Brewing two days a week on his one-barrel brewhouse simply wasn't going to cut it.

The small brewery and taproom has been a welcome addition to an improving downtown Mason City, which has enjoyed the recent opening of the Frank Lloyd Wright Hotel among other notable attractions. With hard work and local investment, the downtown reputation has rebounded, and MCBC has provided respite for locals who wanted to enjoy a beer in a relaxing atmosphere. "Most people that drink craft beer are here to savor it, rather than suck it down," Jake says.

The State Street taproom possesses a relaxed atmosphere without televisions, a bar made from a reclaimed bowling alley, and occasional live music. To honor those who had helped them initiate their dream, the brewery maintains a wall with vintage Polaroid photos of Kickstarter backers—the grassroots "founders" who planted the seed to a blossoming new Mason City hotspot.

A visit to the bar reveals three regular beers, an approachable cream ale, brown porter (Jake's baby), and an IPA, while the other five taps rotate. My tour stumbled across a dark wheat, an ESB, a pale ale, and a black IPA. Jake says his IPA has shifted somewhat in profile from batch to batch, as it was tricky procuring a consistent supply of the same hops in their first year open. He landed a hop contract moving forward, and anticipates dialing his IPA in to his ideal specifications. To satisfy dark beer lovers, MCBC rotates stouts, whether familiar faces like oatmeal stout or dry stout or more creative riffs as was the case on a recent special release for Valentine's Day: a chocolate covered strawberry stout. Brewer's whim rounds out the lineup.

Creative shoestring-budget engineering of elements of the temperature control in their setup have helped MCBC establish themselves while managing costs. Double brewing into two-barrel fermenters means that Jake must brew frequently, but starting small allowed them to commence with both independence and limited debt. "It's a ton of work, but I love it," says Jake.

As patrons have expressed such support, an eye to the future sees the need for increased production. Since space is limited in their current home, the notion of building an offsite production brewery to supply the taproom has been discussed. "We'll have to get bigger," says Jake. "It just has to be the right time and situation."

Brewer Jake Rajewsky toasts the Kickstarter backers pictured on the wall behind him. Their pledges helped make Mason City Brewing Company possible.

The Details

Mason City Brewing Company
28 East State Street
Mason City, Iowa 50401
(641) 423-1080

Online: masoncitybrewing.com
    Facebook, Twitter
Owners: Arian Schuessler,
    Jake Rajewsky, and Justin Merritt
Brewer: Jake Rajewsky
Year opened: 2013
Brewing system: 2-barrel
Tours: Yes
Availability: Taproom draught and growlers
Parking: Street
Awards received: The Brown Porter was named one of the seven best things to eat
    or drink at the Iowa State Fair by chicagoist.com
Year-round beers: Cream Ale, Saison, IPA, and Brown Porter
Food: No, but food trucks are regular in the summertime and local pizza is delivered
    to the taproom free of charge
Local non-beer attractions: Located next to the Historic Park Inn Hotel, the last
    remaining hotel designed by Frank Lloyd Wright. There are numerous tourism
    opportunities available at visitmasoncity.com.
Tip: Brewer Jake Rajewsky favors Mason City's Brown Porter, so that's probably
    a good beer to try.

Notes:

Millstream Brewing Company

Amana

One of Iowa's foremost tourist destinations, the Amana Colonies are a string of seven east-central Iowa villages settled in 1855 by German Pietists. They called themselves die *Gemeinde der wahren Inspiration* (the Community of True Inspiration), and they maintained a communal livelihood until the mid-1930s. While the Amanas are no longer economically independent from the outside world, elements of their former lifeline, specialized handicrafts and farming, are still key to this area's charm. But now, the Colonies, which have been listed as a National Historic Landmark since 1965, sell their wares—handcrafts, furniture, home décor, antiques, wine, and sweets among other items—to a bevy of tourists.

And Amana's *Gemeinde der bier Inspiration*—Millstream Brewing Company—is located at 835 48th Avenue in Amana. Millstream was opened to slake a local beer drought by brothers Carroll F. Zuber, James Roemig, and Dennis Roemig in 1985. The small production brewery added flavor and interest to the Iowa brew scene, but growth has been slow and steady. Another trio, Tom and Teresa Albert and Chris Priebe bought the brewery in 2000, and Chris has headed up efforts in the brewhouse ever since. When they took over, there were sanitation issues to be dealt with, according to Teresa, and she says that they dumped a fair amount of beer as they underwent a deep brewery cleaning to bring the quality up to snuff.

The Albert-Priebe team has been methodical about growth, and for a long time, they functioned on a 15-barrel brewhouse and focused distribution to Iowa only. In 2010, they installed a 20-barrel brewhouse and today, Millstream can be found in neighboring states like Wisconsin, South Dakota, Nebraska, and Minnesota. Year-round offerings include their heavily decorated Vienna-style lager, Schild Brau Amber Lager, along with Windmill Wheat, Back Road Stout and John's Generations White Ale. Millstream also offers a foursome of seasonal releases (Oktoberfest, Hefe"r"weissen, Schokolade Bock, and German Pilsner), as well as a trio of sodas for the non-beer drinkers.

When the Iowa Legislature raised the alcohol by volume limit in 2010, Millstream took advantage of the opportunity to widen their family of beers with a Brewmaster's Extreme Series, which consists of bigger, bolder beers that may or may never be brewed again (a doppelbock and a smoked barley wine are a couple of examples logged in the archives, and brewer's whim dictates the future).

Millstream is a fun visit, as they have a hospitality room with a number of beers flowing and views into the brewhouse, as well as a biergarten for outside imbibing during the warmer months. Among their long list of annual events is the Festival of Iowa Beers, which is a showcase of Iowa brewing talent held each August hosted by the brewery. It's a great event to attend and discover some of the best beers being brewed in Iowa.

Chris has talent, and he has grown the brewery's medal count to 18 national and one international award—to date, they're the state's winningest brewery and a source of pride to many. And from what I've tasted, they deserve it.

The Details

Millstream Brewing Company
835 48th Avenue
Amana, Iowa 52203
(319) 622-3672

Online: millstreambrewing.com, Facebook, Twitter
Owners: Chris Priebe, Teresa Albert, and Tom Albert
Brewmaster: Chris Priebe
Year opened: 1985
Brewing system: 20-barrel
Tours: No
Availability: Currently distributing bottles and kegs in seven states: Iowa, Nebraska, South Dakota, North Dakota, Minnesota, Wisconsin, and Illinois
Parking: Parking lot
Year-round beers: Windmill Wheat, John's White Ale, Schild Brau Amber, Iowa Pale Ale, and Back Road Stout
Seasonal beers: German Pilsner, Hefe"r"weissen, Oktoberfest, and Schokolade Bock

A festival goer peruses the program at Millstream Brewing Company's annual Festival of Iowa Beer in Amana.

Limited release beers: Brewmasters Extreme Series a new beer every 2-3 months—some of these beers will never be brewed again.
Awards: Schild Brau Amber Lager: 16 awards, including gold medals at the World Beer Cup, Great American Beer Festival and Los Angeles International

Commercial Beer Competition; John's White Ale: nine awards, including a gold medal at the LAICBC and silver at GABF; German Pilsner: three awards, including a gold medal at the LAICBC; Back Road Stout: four awards, including LAICBC and GABF gold medals; Windmill Wheat: GABF gold

Events: Maifest in Amana (usually the first weekend of May), live music every Saturday night in the Millsream Biergarten (June-August), Festival of Iowa Beers (Labor Day Weekend), Oktoberfest in Amana (usually the first weekend in October

Food: No

Local non-beer attractions: The Amana Colonies

Tip: Millsteam hosts the annual Festival of Iowa Brewers on Labor Day Weekend. Put it on your to-do list.

Notes:

New American Brewing Company

Ankeny

Owner/Brewmaster David Bryan uses the slogan "a new American tradition" to describe the mentality of Ankeny's New American Brewing Company. But he knows good and well that it's really "an old American tradition." Like so many, he is keen on certain elements of the old days, and he has committed to doing his part to bring them back to life.

"One of the big things that I like about brewing is the history, specifically the American history of brewing," says David. "I like back before Prohibition in the 1800s when every little town had their own brewery. If you traveled to that town, that's what kind of beer you drank — whatever was local. They were mostly small, family-owned businesses, and I was really interested in bringing that tradition back. So New American Brewing Company is where that name came from."

A longtime homebrewer who has surfed the country, living in Kansas, California, Oregon and Colorado before settling in his wife's home state of Iowa, David was inspired by the model of California's Hess Brewing Company and sold his first commercial beer in November of 2012. Working on a two-barrel system to prove the brand and demand, av maintains his day job as a business development manager and spends his evenings cleaning and kegging and weekends brewing.

New American is located in an industrial park just off NE 14th Street (Highway 69) and wouldn't yet characterize itself as a "destination brewery." Nestled into all of 1,200 square feet, Bryan's entire facility is smaller than some larger breweries' fermentation space. (A 600-barrel fermenter, for example, measures 47 by 11.5 feet, and some breweries possess those in double digits.) Despite its nano designation, New American puts out a portfolio of flavorful beers, which are available on draught around Des Moines and Ankeny.

Though there's no taproom (yet), I stopped by so David could show me around and to taste his wares. On my visit, he offered up samples of his Independence Pale Ale, Freedom IPA, 1789 Porter, and Revolution Old Ale. Those are the regulars, but I also scored sneak peeks of Bryan's American Wheat and Classic American Pilsner, both fermenting away, alongside a session IPA.

I joined the 1789 Porter Fan Club. After just a few months in business, the porter distinguished itself as New American's top seller. But David broke my heart (and probably his wife's too, by the sound of it) by predicting that one of his hop-forward offerings will overtake it. I'm not saying they weren't scrumptious, but it's so nice to have a few good dark beers sprinkled about the landscape.

Personal preferences aside, New American provided evidence that Ankeny is to be a notable part of the Iowa craft beer scene. David looks forward to the day when he bumps up in size and adds a taproom and beer garden to the concept, but don't expect New American to ever grow beyond that pre-Prohibition model of each community possessing its own small brewery satisfying a local audience. "I really like the craftsmanship," says David, who doesn't want to become a pencil pushing brewmaster. "I like doing the brewing. I feel like if we got too big I wouldn't be able to enjoy that."

New American's David Bryan takes a break from his brewing duties.

The Details   Notes:

New American Brewing Company
1460 NE 69th Place, Suite 67
Ankeny, Iowa 50021
(515) 250-8703

Online: newamericanbeer.com, Facebook, Twitter
Owners: David Bryan and Tyler Meusburger
Brewmaster: David Bryan
Year opened: 2013
Brewing system: 2-barrel
Tours: Yes
Availability: Draft accounts in Ankeny and Des Moines
Parking: Limited
Year-round beers: Liberty Pale Ale, Freedom IPA, 1789 Porter
Seasonal/limited release beers: Elf's Revenge Winter Warmer, Fall Guy IPA,
    Summer Session IPA, Imperial 1789 Imperial
    Porter, DIPA, BIPA, Sours, and among others
Tip: Try the 1789 Porter!

Number 7 Brewing Company

Ankeny

It was number seven on the list.

After enduring a few layoffs in the corporate world, longtime homebrewer Matt Sims and his wife Jessie sat down to brainstorm a new path. They made a long list of possibilities. Starting a brewery kept coming up in conversations, and they always referred to it as its place on the list. Eventually, all the other prospects fell away and Number 7 Brewing Company was born in June of 2013.

When they first opened up, the Simses integrated another of their interests into the mix—barbecue. They'd competed and catered under the "Bonz-n-Brew BBQ" moniker in the past, and they opened as a full-on brewpub in the former home of Bears, a bar in Old Ankeny. But by September they opted for a re-boot, dropped the kitchen and placed more emphasis on their beer.

Operating with a taproom fueled by a seven-barrel brewing system, Number 7 tries to offer six to seven house beers at any given moment, pours a number of guest beers from other Iowa breweries and maintains a wide assortment of bottled beers in addition to a full bar. Patrons are encouraged to bring food from outside, but beginning in January of 2014, the Simses leased out their kitchen space to Broken Wing Catering. So moving forward, on-site food will be an option while affording Number 7 the opportunity to self distribute their brews to Ankeny and Des Moines bars and restaurants, one of Matt's goals of the operation.

Having worked for a stint at Court Avenue Restaurant and Brewing Company, Matt heads up the brewing duties, though he has a trio of homebrewers that also contribute to the brewhouse. In addition to the seven-barrel brewhouse, Number 7 pilots beers on a one-barrel system to keep the taps fresh and imbibers on their toes. If patrons respond to a pilot batch, Number 7 will produce a big batch to meet demand. Matt places emphasis on three core beers: Number 7 American Amber Ale, Drunken Sailor IPA and Cocoa Bessie Chocolate Milk Stout. Every Saturday, a new small batch beer is released.

On my visit, he also had a raspberry wheat and a maple nut brown ale. The latter was called "It's a Bit Nutty," and house rules require the customer to order it in a British accent. Jessie was a stickler, and so everyone at the bar donned their best Austin Powers imitations and took advantage of the icebreaker to have a good time. Together. Which is what you're supposed to do at a bar. And in Ankeny, you can do that at Number 7.

The Details

Number 7 Brewing Company
302 SW Maple Street
Ankeny, Iowa 50023
(515) 964-5240

Online: number7brewing.com, Facebook
Owners: Matt and Jessie Sims
Year opened: 2013
Tours: No
Availability: Draught onsite
Parking: Street
Year-round beers: Number 7 American Amber Ale, Drunken Sailor IPA and Cocoa Bessie Chocolate Milk Stout
Seasonal/limited release beers: Rotate with brewer's whim
Food: Catered onsite
Local non-beer attractions: Saylorville Recreation Area, Big Creek State Park, High Trestle Trail, historic uptown shopping, and 10 minutes from downtown Des Moines
Did you know? Number 7 Brewing Company was Ankeny's first brewery.

Notes:

Okoboji Brewing Company

Spirit Lake

Founded in July of 2009 by the father-son team of Donn and Cole Martens, Okoboji Brewing Company (OBC) has taken a baby-steps approach to brewery ownership. Longtime fans of beer and brewing, the Martenses partnered with homebrewer Erik DeKeyzer to enter the market in 2011 by contract brewing beers at Great River Brewery in Davenport. The move helped OBC establish its brands before outlaying cash for every element of the brewery buildout.

In November of 2012, OBC moved into its permanent home at 3705 Highway 71 in Spirit Lake. There, DeKeyzer rounded out the taproom offerings on a one-barrel pilot system, while elements of the planned 25-barrel brewhouse came together piece by piece. I paid Cole a visit in early 2014, and he noted that installing the brewery's glycol system was the final piece of the puzzle to gain complete independence from contract brewing and begin producing their Boji Beach Golden Rye Ale, Boji Blue Pale Ale, and Midwest Charm Farmhouse Ale.

Not long after DeKeyzer stepped away from the brewhouse to allow brewer Jared White to take over OBC's brewing, I bellied up to the custom butternut bar to try three pilot beers: Vanilla Cream Stout, American IPA and West Okoboji Cream Ale. All were engaging examples of beers that Jared will be churning out, but the West Okoboji Cream Ale was particularly so.

It came about when an Omaha, Nebraska-based homebrewer stopped by to purchase some ingredients (OBC diversifies its income by selling homebrew supplies out of the taproom). It turns out that this gentleman was in the neighborhood cultivating wild yeast for a planned homebrew. The Martenses encouraged him bring in a sample so that they could toy with the local yeast themselves. He obliged and the cream ale was Jared's first batch utilizing the strain. Rather than the typical, rather pedestrian character found in a cream ale, the OBC experiment revealed a nuanced American wild ale. Cole speculates that the yeast will make its way into a Berliner Weisse-inspired beer in the future.

In addition to the tone set by the gorgeous bar, the taproom itself has a cozy feel that Cole describes as "Camp Endless Summer." Keeping the lake-driven summer tourism in mind, OBC's concept was to make a summer camp for adults in the drinking space. But, Cole says, that doesn't mean that kids aren't welcome. As the lakes area is a family-oriented destination, so is OBC. The taproom has board games and house-made sarsaparilla so that a cool drink after a day at the beach can be fun for the whole family.

The Details

Okoboji Brewing Company
3705 Highway 71
Spirit Lake, Iowa 51360
(712) 336-8406

Online: brewokoboji.com, Facebook
Owners: Donn Martens, Cole Martens, and Eric DeKeyzer
Brewmaster: Jared White
Year opened: 2012
Brewing System: 25-Barrel
Tours: Yes
Availability: Draught and 32- and 64-ounce growlers at the taproom; 4-packs of 16-ounce cans in Iowa, Nebraska, and South Dakota
Parking: Parking lot and street
Public Transportation: taxi (seasonal)
Year-round beers: Boji Beach Golden Rye Ale, Boji Blue Pale Ale, and Midwest Charm Farmhouse Ale
Seasonal/limited release beers: Shot in the Dark Vanilla Cream Stout, Bandwagon American IPA, and Kolsch; Sarsaparilla
Food: None, but patrons are welcome to bring/order in.
Local non-beer attractions: Fishing, boating, and other lake activities
Did you know?: Okoboji Brewing Company brews a wild ale with yeast harvested along the shores of nearby Lake Okoboji.

Notes:

Old Man River Restaurant and Brewery

McGregor

Allison and Angelica Dayrit-Roberts were customers at Old Man River Restaurant and Brewery in McGregor for five years before taking over management in 2012. When they first discovered Old Man River, they'd recently moved from Los Angeles, California to western Wisconsin to tend a property that Allison's parents had purchased to live on and work during their impending retirement. Allison and Angelica established an organic farm and fruit orchards there, and spent their free time exploring the vicinity, which included the historic river town of McGregor.

They appreciated the vibe and history of Old Man River, but when the management opportunity came about, the northeast Iowa brewpub was in the midst of transition. Brewmaster Jake Simmons had departed to establish Backpocket Brewing Company, a production brewery in Coralville, and Old Man River's eight-barrel brewhouse had been placed on hiatus. While they sought a brewhouse solution, Allison and Angelica focused on the kitchen and dining service to contribute to the interest of McGregor's cluster of interesting boutiques and artists that have been working to reinvent the community and complement its proximity to both historical and outdoor recreation opportunities.

Allison and Angelica did not inherit a blank canvas. Old Man River is housed in the former office and living space of "Diamond Jo" Reynolds, who built the structure in the mid- to late-1880s to serve as the headquarters for his successful riverboat passenger service and fur and grain trading business. In addition to historical photos documenting the story of yesteryear, the door to his vault, as well as a bust of the successful entrepreneur, are on display in the dining room, which has also seen incarnations as a post office, gift shop, winery, pizza parlor, bank, and apartment building in its lifetime.

Allison appreciates Diamond Jo's spirit of entrepreneurship and hopes to channel that into jumpstarting success in his former office space. After pursuing a number of avenues toward renewed on-site brewing, Allison and Angelica worked out an agreement in late March of 2014 that brought Jake back into the picture to train Allison and Angelica, along with a newly-hired assistant brewer on the McGregor system to collaborate on an ongoing basis to bring both variety and quality to both breweries' taprooms.

The first step of Old Man River's new beer lineup came on April 22, 2014, when Old Man River tapped the first of these collaborations, a lightly hopped amber ale. Plans (and beers) continue to unfold on a day-by-day basis, but one thing is for certain: McGregor beer is back at Old Man River Brewing Company.

The Details

Old Man River Restaurant & Brewery
123 A. Street
McGregor, Iowa 52157
(563) 873-1999

Online: oldmanriverbrewery.com,
   Facebook
Owners: Dave and Marci Strutt
Operators: Allison and Angelica
   Dayrit-Roberts
Brewster: Allison Dayrit-Roberts
Year opened: 2008
Brewing system: 8.5-barrel
Tour info: Yes
Availability: On-site service only
Parking: Street and private lot
   (RV, boat, and trailer accessible)
Year-round beers: To be determined
Seasonal/limited release beers: To be
   determined
Annual events: Oktoberfest
Food: Infused Modern American
Local non-beer attractions: Pikes Peak
State Park, Villa Louis Historical Site,
   and Effigy Mounds National Monument

McGregor's Old Man River Brewing Company offers fresh beer in a lovely northeast Iowa setting.

Tip: Take time to explore the natural beauty surrounding Old Man River—it's
   a beautiful part of the state!

Notes:

Olde Main Brewing Company

Ames

It was a hot summer day, and I'd just finished a hike with the family. "Boy, I sure could go for a cool drink!" I said. "What about you guys?" This was my sneaky way of paying Olde Main Brewing Company a visit, since it was "in the neighborhood." My wife saw right through my ploy, but my two boys were just happy to visit civilization and sling back a root beer.

There are two pieces to the Olde Main puzzle, the pub and the restaurant. We sat down to cool off on the pub-side, and I worked my way through a sampler. During that visit, I really enjoyed a one-off offering, Tongue Punch IPA. I heard there were no plans to brew the beer again, which is about how my luck runs.

While I've always thought that Olde Main's addition of chamomile was a nice aromatic twist to their Dinkey Wheat (essentially a Belgian witbier), I usually turn to the Off KILTer Scottish Ale. Both are decidedly different from that pint of Tongue Punch, but the threesome marks waypoints of where the Olde Main family of beers might tread. Other year-round beers that Brewmaster John Rundall provides to consumers not only on draught at the brewery but also in bottles around Iowa are Long Face Amber Ale, Clone American Pale Ale, and Sodbuster Stout.

The pub provides a comfortable drinking area with both barspace and booths, as well as an upstairs seating area that looks down on the bar. The 15-barrel brewhouse is visible through glass behind the bar. There are video games and tabletop shuffleboard to keep the kids entertained if you stop by after a Saturday hike like me, though these kinds of recreation are great for kids of all ages.

If you're meeting friends for a meal, you may want to find a table on the restaurant side of the establishment, which has a second bar at the ready. The menu ranges from hand-cut steaks to vegetarian dishes, and also includes gluten-free offerings. Both sides provide a good atmosphere for friends and beverages, whether you're in town to watch the Cyclones play or to do a little shopping in downtown Ames.

The Details

Olde Main Brewing Company
316 Main Street
Ames, Iowa 50010
(515) 232-0553

A bird's eye view of the bar and brewhouse at Olde Main Brewing Company in Ames.

Online: oldemainbrewing.com, Facebook, Twitter

Owner: Scott Griffen

Brewmaster: John R. Rundall

Year opened: 2004

Brewing system: 15-barrel

Tours: Yes

Availability: On-site draught and growlers; 12-ounce bottles and draught throughout Iowa

Parking: On- and off-street parking

Public Transportation: Taxi, Cyride

Year-round beers: Dinkey Wheat®, Long Face Amber Ale, Off KILTer Scottish Ale, Clone APA, Gryphonbrau Premium Lager, and Sodbuster Stout

Seasonal/limited release beers: Elkman Milk Stout, Lucky Shillelagh Irish Red, Lemontyme Lemon Ale, Der Festen Oktoberfest, Horseman's Revenge Pumpkin Spice Ale, and Reindeer Fuel Chocolate Porter, as well as a lineup of brewpub exclusives

Food: Hand-cut steaks, burgers, etc., including gluten-free and vegetarian offerings

Local non-beer attractions: Iowa State University athletics, Black's Heritage Farm, Reiman Gardens

Tip: In addition to a restaurant and a family of bottled and kegged beers, Olde Main provides catering services.

Notes

Peace Tree Brewing Company

Knoxville

Named for the historic tree located near the town of Red Rock—now Lake Red Rock—Peace Tree Brewing Company serves the Knoxville community in much the way that the famous sycamore tree once did. Its taproom serves as a meeting place. A few generations ago, those converging were Native Americans and fur traders. Treaties are said to have been negotiated at this landmark. Today, those congregating at Peace Tree are united in their love of good beer.

That's the old-school back story, but the formation of the brewery itself provides an interesting tale. Peace Tree is not the tale of a homebrewer-turned-pro like happens so often today. It is the story of a Knoxville family that sought a purpose for an extra property they owned. They were not beer geeks; they were insurance folk. Dan McKay, Megan McKay, and Scott Ziller brainstormed a use for their Main Street property—the former home to a Nash Rambler dealership. Among the ideas floating about the room was a craft brewery, a concept growing in popularity. Though Scott had dabbled in homebrewing, he wasn't so deep in the culture that this was a pet project to suit his private dreams. The trio set out to educate themselves on the business end of beer, attending the Craft Brewers Conference to feel out the idea. Enamored by the positive vibe of the industry, Dan, Megan and Scott launched Peace Tree Brewing Company in 2009.

They brought Brewmaster Joe Kesteloot on board to oversee brewing operations. Given free reign to create a family of beers, Joe toyed with formulas on a 10-gallon setup while the 20-barrel brewhouse build-out came to life. From those early days of experimentation came Red Rambler, a malt-leaning amber ale; Hop Wrangler, a multinational take on the IPA style; Rye Porter, a dark-and-spicy brew that is no longer a full-timer; and Blonde Fatale, a bold Belgian Blonde Ale which earned a coveted gold medal at the World Beer Cup competition in April of 2014. Of the four beers, only Red Rambler is free of a Belgian yeast dose, which twists the beers from "normal" style parameters ever so slightly.

But this Knoxville crew isn't normal. Peace Tree carries a style of its own in every element of its being. The beers maintain a twist. The branding is hip and eye-catching.

And the bottles are short-and-stubby and out of the ordinary. Everything about Peace Tree sets itself apart, and the brewery has enjoyed phenomenal success as a result. Only four years out of the gates, Peace Tree has expanded its footprint not only across Iowa, but also into Minnesota, Nebraska, and Kansas, causing capacity issues. At the time of this writing, expansion plans are in the works to help Peace Tree meet demand for their products.

One step that has already been taken was the summer 2013 addition of Sidekick Kolsch to Peace Tree's seasonal lineup. Joe traveled to his alma mater, Cold Spring Brewery in Minnesota, to brew and package the new summer release aimed at the outdoorsy market. Packaged in 12-ounce cans, Sidekick marks Peace Tree's first foray into the aluminum packaging sector, making it great for the beach, golf course and campsite while reducing the negative sway of oxygen and light on the beer, as well as easing the environmental impact. In late 2013, Peace Tree followed with a new line of 22-ounce specialty bottles in the form of their first serious release of a barrel-aged beer, their Templeton Red, which was a Templeton Rye barrel-aged version of their Red Rambler. Joe nailed it on both releases.

With a tenacious work ethic and a pile of talent in-house, the Peace Tree beers are delicious — and notable — within their home state of Iowa and a good deal further afield. Couple that with the company's community-minded generosity, and the success is well deserved. Rest assured, these fun-lovers have more surprises up their sleeves.

The Details

Peace Tree Brewing Company
107 W. Main St.
Knoxville, Iowa 50138
(641) 842-2739

Online: peacetreebrewing.com, Facebook, Twitter
Owners: Dan McKay, Megan McKay, and Scott Ziller
Brewmaster: Joe Kesteloot
Year opened: 2009
Brewing system: 20-barrel
Tours: Yes
Availability: Bottles and draught in Iowa, Minnesota, Kansas, and Nebraska
Parking: Street
Awards received: 2014 World Beer Cup Gold Medal andNorth American Brewer's Association 2011 bronze medal for Blonde Fatale, Edible Iowa River Valley 2011 Local Hero Award for Artisan Beverage, Des Moines CityView "Best Type of Beer" 2013 and "Best Locally Brewed Beer" for 2012 and 2013
Year-round beers: Blonde Fatale (Belgian Strong Ale), Red Rambler (American Amber Ale), Hop Wrangler IPA (Belgo-American IPA), and Root Beer

Seasonal/limited release beers: Hop Sutra (Double IPA), Cornucopia (Saison), No Coast IPA (American IPA), Rye Porter, Black River Gumbo (Stout), Imperial Stout, Sidekick Kolsch (German Kolsch-style Ale), Templeton Red (Barrel-aged Amber Ale), and Indecision Dark IPA

Annual Events: Brews & Muse—an annual block party held late September

Food: Carryout menus from local restaurants are available

Local non-beer attractions: National Sprint Car Hall of Fame and Museum, Lake Red Rock, Birthplace of the Iowa Flag

Tip: Blonde Fatale isn't the "light beer" that many imbibers think it is—it's an 8.5% ABV Strong Belgian Blonde Ale that deserves respect (and restraint).

Notes:

A camera crew films footage of Peace Tree brewer Joe Kesteloot's barrel program

Raccoon River Brewing Company

Des Moines

It may seem an odd seasonal beer to covet—imperial stouts usually get that honor—but one of the beers I most look forward to returning each year is Raccoon River Brewing Company's maibock. One, it harkens the return of spring—*Mai* is German for May—and two, it's delicious. It's a malty, pale golden lager with a hint more hop character than most bocks, and for me, it really bridges the gap between beers meant for the cold days of winter and those that have a different job to do during the hot days of summer.

And it's a good example of Brewmaster Dave Coy's talent. A stovetop brewer in his college days at Iowa State University, Dave moved to Colorado and went to work in the brewing industry at Denver's Wynkoop Brewing Company. In 1997, the Wynkoop group wanted to open a second location in Des Moines, and Dave returned to his native state to take the helm at the 10th and Mulberry brewpub.

There are similarities between the two. While good food and beer are prerequisites, both have dining upstairs and down, inhabit characterful downtown buildings with flashes of wood, brass and brewhouses visible behind glass, offer space for private parties, and both possess ample billiards space on the upper floor.

In 2000, Raccoon River's largest local investor, E. Jeffrey Hunter, took over sole ownership of the well-regarded Des Moines brewpub.

Dave brews five year-round beers—Tallgrass Light, Vanilla Cream Ale, Homestead Red, Bandit IPA, Stonecutter Stout—as well as a root beer and a cream soda for the kids. For its smooth texture and coffee notes, I repeatedly reach for the Stonecutter. But that's just me. Dave's cultivated a lot of Bandit fans, as well. Seasonals range from a Pilsner to an imperial stout, and all of Dave's offerings have a strong match for food, a passion of the brewer who can often be found helping out in the kitchen during the downtown pub's lunch rush.

In his tenure at Raccoon River, the tireless advocate of Iowa beer and longtime president of the Iowa Brewers Guild has seen a lot of changes in the Iowa brewing scene. When he arrived in his Des Moines brewhouse, he was one of but a handful of Iowa brewers. Today, he's an elder in a fifty-deep pack of quality beer producers. And as long as he keeps putting out that maibock each spring, we'll all have something to look forward to.

The Details

Raccoon River Brewing Company
200 Tenth Street
Des Moines, Iowa 50309
(515) 362-5222

Online: raccoonbrew.com, Facebook, Twitter
Owner: E. Jeffrey Hunter
Brewmaster: David Coy
Year opened: 1997
Brewing system: 15-barrel
Tours: Yes
Availability: Draught onsite, with a few local draught accounts. Growlers available.
Parking: On-street parking available and several nearby parking garages.
Public Transportation: In the heart of Downtown Des Moines, so ample public transportation available.
Year-round beers: Tallgrass Light, Vanilla Cream Ale, Homestead Red, Bandit IPA, Stonecutter Stout
Seasonal/limited release beers: Always rotating and coming up with new beers.
Food: Contemporary American pub fare with a few interesting ethnic flourishes
Local non-beer attractions: Everything available in the capital city of the state.
Tip: Seriously, you should try to catch Dave's maibock!

Notes:

Brewer Dave Coy's boots stand at the ready at Raccoon River Brewing Company in Des Moines.

Rock Bottom Restaurant and Brewery

West Des Moines

My first craft beer experience in Iowa took place about seven years ago at the West Des Moines location of Rock Bottom Restaurant and Brewery. There are thirty-eight Rock Bottoms sprinkled from sea to shining sea, and if I carried any trepidation about my visit, it was because I was walking into a "chain," something that I'm usually keen to avoid.

The first Rock Bottom opened at the base of the Prudential Building (the bottom of the rock) in downtown Denver, Colorado, in 1991. Founder Frank Day built a successful business, and the brewpub would be replicated again and again around the country, with the West Des Moines location opening in August of 1997 and Regional Brewmaster Eric Sorensen taking over the brewhouse in 2004.

What I found at Rock Bottom, the one in West Des Moines as well as at the others I've visited in other parts of the country, is that this string of brewpubs lives up to its tagline: "Serious about our food. Crazy about our beer."

On that first visit to the West Des Moines location, I sat down to seven samples and an order of smoked salmon fish and chips (though over the years I've had my fair share of Bourbonzola Burgers), was pleased with both the quality and range of beers on offer, and have stopped being so judgmental of restaurants with more than one location. Who am I to criticize a successful business model? As long as it involves high quality beers, I no longer care. And Rock Bottom does good work, both in the brewhouse and in the kitchen.

I must confess, however, that over the years I've become not only acquainted with, but a friend and collaborator with Eric. My first book, *Diary of a Part-Time Monk*, told the story of our 2011 historical research into the doppelbock style of beer. We've brewed together. We've shared meals together. We've done radio interviews together. And we earned a silver medal at the Festival of Wood and Barrel-Aged Beers in Chicago for our Barrel Reserve Illuminator Doppelbock.

On one hand, the reader may wish to take my discussion of this brewpub with a giant grain of salt. I'm a friend of the brewer and have some emotional attachment to at least one beer that I have the privilege of helping to brew on a now-annual basis. If the reader chooses to ignore me, I'll understand. But on the other hand, I wasn't Eric's comrade when I first posted an online review back on June 19, 2007. I was a discriminating beer drinker in search of both epiphanies and flaws at every bend of the elbow.

What I found was a stable of solid beers. And that remains the case today, even after a 2010 merger that brought Rock Bottom into the CraftWorks family along with Old Chicago Restaurants, and Gordon Biersch Brewery Restaurants.

Following the merger, there were changes. The Lumpy Dog Brown disappeared, much to the chagrin of local imbibers. And a core lineup of four beers emerged with all Rock Bottom locations utilizing the same formula: RB Kölsch, RB White, RB IPA, and RB Red. But after that, the brewers have the freedom to do whatever they wish. Eric has sixteen taps, and he brews a wide range of rotating beers to keep beer enthusiasts exploring, throwing down an assortment of stouts and IPAs, barrel-aged delights, wild ales, obscure styles like Grodziskie, and beers brewed with the likes of lavender, chilis, hempseeds and evergreen boughs. In his nine years at the helm, Eric's brewed over a hundred unique beers and gained well-deserved respect within the Iowa beer scene.

If a visit to Rock Bottom is to provide a pensive takeaway, it's this: keep an open mind about what you're drinking—and an open mind about the company producing it.

The Details

Rock Bottom Restaurant and Brewery
4508 University Avenue
West Des Moines, Iowa 50266
(515) 267-8900

Online: rockbottom.com, Facebook, Twitter, Beermenus.com
Owners: Centerbridge Partners d.b.a. CraftWorks Restaurants & Breweries
Brewmaster: Eric Sorensen
Year opened: 1997
Brewing system: 8-10-barrel
Availability: On-site and a few local draught accounts
Parking: Parking lot
Public Transportation: Bus
Awards received: Barrel Reserve Illuminator Dopplebock (2011 Silver Medal Winner, Festival of Wood & Barrel Aged Beers: Strong/Double/Imperial Dark Category), Sticke Alt (2010 Bronze Medal Award Winner, Great American Beer Festival®; German-Style Altbier), Bourbon Fest (2009 Silver Medal Winner, Festival of Wood and Barrel Aged Beers; Classic Styles); Roggenbier (2004 Silver Medal Award Winner, Great American Beer Festival®; German-Style Rye Beer), and Large Brewpub & Large Brewpub Brewer of the Year (GABF 2008 and 2013)
Year-Round Beers: RB Kölsch, RB White, RB IPA and RB Red
Seasonal/limited release beers: In addition to the four core beers, Rock Bottom opens up creativity to its brewers. At any time, patrons at the West Des Moines location will find 16 beers on tap. Sorensen has brewed over 100 unique beer styles in his tenure as brewmaster.

Special Events: Charity tapping events: Rocktoberfest, Winter Tartan, Fire Chief, Summer Honey, Stand Up Guy (also Golf Outing that has raised over $100K for Iowa Homeless Youth Centers)

Food: American featuring Southwest-inspired specials and a full bar

Local non-beer attractions: Living History Farms, Blank Park Zoo, Jordan Creek Mall, Menace Soccer, Buccaneers Hockey, Raccoon River, Des Moines River, and bike trails

Tip: A rare treat in even the best beer bars, Rock Bottom often has cask ales on tap.

Notes:

Brewer Eric Sorensen takes in the aroma while brewing a batch of beer.

Rustic Brew
Hampton

Walk in the door at 117 1st Street NW in Hampton, and you'll be pleased to have entered a coffee shop just packed with character. With hardwood floors and exposed brick walls laden with murals, the space is an ideal location for a cup of coffee and conversation. But there's more.

For Joel Heuer, homebrewing was a hobby that mushroomed, and eventually, it melded with his wife's interest in opening a business. Joel and Kathy Heuer teamed up with friends Brad and Kim Mulford in January of 2013 to purchase an existing coffee shop, but they brought in their own ideas, adding value in the form of Joel's beers in June of the same year (as well as locally produced wines), to make Rustic Brew a unique concept within Iowa's beer scene.

The result is a café/brewpub that serves coffee, sandwiches, beer and native wines in a pleasant atmosphere that welcomes a wide range of clientele. While I visited, I saw a late-morning coffee group playing cards and surveying the small town news. Later in the day, Joel says, the beverages of choice shift, but the enthusiasm for conversation remains much the same. Rustic Brew provides a backdrop for couples to enjoy a drink after work without the stigma attached to "going to the bar," as can sometimes be the case in smaller towns. A school employee by day, Joel is sensitive to this vibe, and Rustic Brew ably combats it.

RB is not a bar. It's a gathering place, whether one's thirsty for coffee, wine, or beer. Hungry? The café also serves an assortment of paninis, and the local favorite, a reuben sandwich.

Joel's half-barrel brewing system resides upstairs in a space that might otherwise be utilized as an apartment. There, Joel, a school liaison officer and longtime football coach, brews up small batches of three standard beers, his Slobber Knocker Oatmeal Stout, Wood Cellar Blonde Ale, and Old Man River Citrus Wheat. He rounds out his network of six taps with rotating beers, that, on my visit, included Slightly Off-"Kilt"er Irish Red Ale, RB 4:05 Amber Ale, and Twisted Pilsner.

Well received by the community of 4,500 residents, Joel's beers have been popular since the taps started flowing, and he struggles to keep up with demand. As a result, Joel says he'll give up his longtime high school coaching gig in the fall of 2014 to help grow and develop Rustic Brew.

The Details

Rustic Brew
117 1st Street
Hampton, Iowa 50441
(641) 456-2141

Online: www.rusticbrew.com, Facebook
Owners: Joel and Kathy Heuer/Brad and Kim Mulford
Brewmaster: Joel Heuer
Year opened: 2013
Brewing System: 15-gallon
Tours: Yes
Availability: Draught, growlers and Boston rounds sold on-site
Parking: Street
Year-Round Beers: Wood Cellar Blonde Ale, Old Man River Citrus Wheat,
    Slobber Knocker Oatmeal Stout, and Slightly Off-"Kilt"er Smoked Irish Red Ale
Seasonal/Limited Release Beers: Pumpkin Ale
Food: Sandwiches, etc.
Local Non-Beer Attractions: Franklin County Fair (mid-July)
Tip: In addition to local beer, Rustic Brew also serves native wines.

Notes:

SingleSpeed Brewing Company

Cedar Falls

SingleSpeed Brewing Company owner/brewmaster Dave Morgan spent the first 16 years of his post-collegiate life in the restaurant industry "serving beer, drinking beer, and then serving some more beer." It won't be a stretch to believe that a beer enthusiast like Dave might use that time to conceptualize his own place, and open it in the shadow of his alma mater, the University of Northern Iowa.

As the name and logo suggest, Dave is an avid cyclist, and as I sat and sampled beers on a bustling Saturday night, I couldn't help but imagine that this would have been the brewery I'd love to have opened with an old gradeschool/cycling buddy of mine. Thanks to Dave, I'm able to enjoy the concept without all the work.

Hardwood floors, exposed brick walls, and framed bike art showcase the character of the Main Street building, while presenting a clean and pleasing atmosphere for a night out with friends. Above the bar, amber-glowing growler pendants provide ambient light with a branded touch. Behind the bar, a huge chalkboard presents the taplist, while a wooden library ladder stands at the ready if the bartender needs to change the list or retrieve a bottle of wine or liquor from on high.

In addition to the seven SingleSpeed beers and five guest taps pouring on the day of my visit, Dave, ever the supporter of all things local, had eight wines from two Iowa wineries and a 15-strong lineup of various spirits from three Iowa distilleries. I wouldn't call SingleSpeed a full-blown brewpub but they do offer a limited selection of rotating appetizers, which is described as "a revolving menu of food assembled for the sole purpose of pairing with our ales." For example: the IPA Blanco-brined, dry-rubbed wings with salsa verde cream is recommended to accompany their SingleHop Chinook IPA.

The beer geek might be curious about SingleSpeed's standard lineup. Well, they don't do that. Seasonal and limited release beers are the basis of their operation. Crafting beers on a three-barrel brewhouse, Dave manages to have something for everyone. On a cold night in January, I tasted SnowShoe '14 (a winter warmer), SnowBike '14 (Belgo-IPA), HopHefe, Saison, Belgian Pale Ale, SingleHop Chinook, and Cocoa Raspberry Porter. Were I to return a month later, those beers are likely to be but memories.

Offering locally crafted beers that he wants to brew when he wants to brew them, Dave fills an artisanal niche within Cedar Falls' downtown area and a flavorful wayside for the beer adventurer on the hunt.

The Details

SingleSpeed Brewing Company
128 Main Street
Cedar Falls, Iowa 50613

Online: singlespeedbrewing.com,
  Facebook, Twitter
Owner/Brewmaster: Dave Morgan
Opened: 2012
Brewing system: 3-barrel
Tours: Yes
Availability: Taproom only
Parking: Lot to the East, on-street parking
Year-round beers: N/A
Seasonal/limited release beers: Their primary line of business
Annual events: Iowa Games SnowShoe/SnowBike Competition (SingleSpeed
  brews two beers exclusively for this event each year)
Food: Flatbreads, dips, wings, etc. in a revolving menu of small plates assembled for
  the sole purpose of pairing with house ales
Local non-beer attractions: UNI Panthers, Waterloo Black Hawks
Tip: Check out the menu, which rotates frequently to match foods with the day's
  current lineup of beers.

Notes:

Sutliff Cider Company

Lisbon

If you're looking for a beautiful setting to kick back with a drink and listen to local music, look no further than Sutliff Cider Company (SCC). That's right—cider company. It's not a brewery, but it deserves mention in this book, because craft beer and cider are friends.

Located in east-central Iowa about two miles south of Lisbon on Sutliff Road, SCC is the fruit of owner/cidermaker Scott Ervin's toil. An engineer by trade, Scott opened the cidery in 2002 after migrating to Iowa from Los Angeles. He bought an acreage where he found an apple orchard onsite, but, a beer lover with the idea of opening a brewery and utilizing as many locally-grown ingredients as possible in that endeavor, he promptly planted hops in the ground.

However, he wasn't afraid of putting those apples to use. "But how many apple pies can you make?" he says, on his transition from baking with apples to pressing and fermenting them. Scott fell in love with his bone-dry creations—ultra-refreshing on a hot summer day—and decided to alter his trajectory toward cider production.

The 600 trees that Scott now maintains on the property only produce enough cider to last two to four weeks, and so he sources apples (Jonathan, Gala, Cortland, and Macintosh, among others) from a number of local orchards, as well as from Michigan when the local apple-coffers run dry. Scott and his staff produce in the neighborhood of one hundred thousand gallons of cider per year, which is available not only at the facility, but also around the state on draught and in 750-milliliter bottles.

For the first couple of years, guests could sit under tents and drink Scott's cider outside the building that he dedicated to production, but eventually—over the course of three winters—Scott renovated his barn, which was built in the late 1880s or early 1890s. Soaked with character, the barn/tasting room opened in 2008 and provides a rustic backdrop for sipping and relaxing. It has become a popular destination for both locals and drinkers traveling from further afield to investigate the notable (and only) Iowa cider producer.

Typically, SCC is only open to the public on Saturdays and Sundays (April-October), but it's located in such a picturesque setting that for the 2014 season, wedding bookings have usurped all of the Saturday drinking sessions from thirsty patrons. While this may be disappointing for some, one look at the cidery's digs, and it's easy to see why the pergola that Scott built has become such a popular wedding site. Sundays, however, still bring joy to the broader public. Along with SCC's signature cider, imbibers can enjoy food, live music and both indoor and outdoor seating.

The renovation of the barn was no small task, as it still had mangers in place and dirt floors. With low ceilings, all the preliminary dirt work had to be done by hand before cement could be poured and stained to set the base of the taproom. Over-head, log beams—bark and all—are visible, while original stonework adds to the character. Bar stools are made from retired barrel staves. French oak wine barrels filled with cider (aged for roughly six months) are stacked all about.

It's a gorgeous setting to yield to the charisma of Scott's ciders, which aren't quite as dry as his original elixirs—he back-sweetens them slightly. Rounded by acidity through careful blending of apple varieties and lightly carbonated, Scott's cider (SCC primarily offers one product, though Scott ex-periments with drier versions and the occasional integration of other fruits) pairs well with lighter fair and makes a wonderful quencher on its own.

Scott Ervin pours a glass of Lisbon's finest: Sutliff Hard Cider.

For those looking for a change of pace or in need of a gluten-free offering, SCC is ideally and deservedly established for cider's recent revival alongside craft beer. But if you're dead-set on drinking a beer, Scott maintains a few guest taps with Iowa beers pouring as well. So everyone can be happy.

The Details

Sutliff Cider Company
382 Sutliff Road
Lisbon, Iowa 52253
(319) 455-4093

Online: sutliffcider.com, Facebook
Owner/Cidermaker: Scott Ervin
Year opened: 2002
Tours: No
Availability: Draught and 750-mililiter
  bottles throughout Iowa
Parking: Lot
Year-round offering: Sutliff Cider
Seasonal/limited releases: Not so much, but a few cider riffs may emerge
Food: Yes
Local non-cider (or beer) attraction: Sutliff Bridge
Tip: Sutliff Cider Company offers live music on Sundays, from 3-6 p.m.
  (April-October).

Notes:

Third Base Sports Bar and Brewery

Cedar Rapids

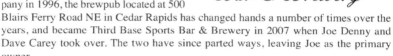

Originating as Cedar Brewing Company in 1996, the brewpub located at 500 Blairs Ferry Road NE in Cedar Rapids has changed hands a number of times over the years, and became Third Base Sports Bar & Brewery in 2007 when Joe Denny and Dave Carey took over. The two have since parted ways, leaving Joe as the primary owner.

With 42 televisions, including one at every single booth, Third Base is a great place to catch a game. According to Head Brewer Travis Scheidecker it wasn't always the best place for a beer, but a trial by fire in the world of professional brewing—which included a lot of support from other brewers—and the Third Base beers have gained solid footing and a respected place within the Iowa beer scene.

At the age of 25, Travis took over the brewer's position on a whim in 2005. "If I would have had any idea [what I was signing up for]," he says. "I wouldn't have volunteered. I was completely ignorant."

The former brewer had departed, and without so much as a five-gallon batch of homebrew under his belt, Travis agreed to take on the brewing duties at a staff meeting. It was an upward step in pay, sounded like fun, and fit with Travis' schooling at the time—he was enrolled in culinary school at Kirkwood Community College.

A consultant came in to provide support, which amounted to five 17-hour days of teaching Travis how to safely move liquid around the brewery and how to safely use the chemicals and gas involved in brewing. Teaching Travis how to make beer wouldn't make it to the agenda. Time and budget constraints limited the consultation to equipment use and safety.

From there on, Travis was on his own. "I started buying books and listening to podcasts to learn to brew, figuring out what to do every day as I went," he says, of his labor to become a competent brewer.

Enter homebrewers and other colleagues within the industry. Travis found abundant support at his fingertips. "I didn't even know what to ask for," he recalls, but a number of individuals availed themselves to help with cleaning, brewing and recipe formulation as Travis worked to learn the craft.

Nearly 10 years later, Travis has gained a wealth of knowledge, producing notable beers and gaining the respect of both customers and his peers. I visited the brewery on a bustling Saturday night, and found five core beers on tap: Golden Hawk Wheat, Red

Rocket Amber Ale, Bees Knees Honey Ale, Flying Aces Pale Ale, and Black Cobra Oatmeal Stout.

In addition to these, I found myself trying his Irish red ale and a smoked porter, as well as a "multi-grain ale" utilizing Horizon and Citra hops straight from the fermenter. Travis described it as a "shot in the dark recipe," as he created the beer on a whim. "Some days we have a fermenter open, and we're thinking, what are we going to put in there? So I just whip up a recipe the day before or that morning, and we throw it in there and see what happens." This beer worked, a shoot-from-the-hip example of all that Travis has learned over the years, thanks to the freedom afforded him by his employers. "It's a great educational platform," Travis says. "I can do anything I want."

Brewer Travis Scheidecker explores the nose on a beer during the barrel aging process.

What he wanted to do from the start was make beer. Then he wanted to make it better. And a taste at the source will reveal that all his hard work and late nights have paid off.

The Details

Third Base Sports Bar & Brewery
500 Blairs Ferry NE
Cedar Rapids, Iowa 52402
(319)-378-9090

Online: 3rdbasebrewery.com, Facebook
Owner: Joe Denny
Brewmaster: Travis Scheidecker

Year opened: 1996

Brewing system: 10-barrel system, brewing 8.5-barrel batches due to the size of their serving tanks.

Tours: Yes

Availability: Draught at the brewpub only

Parking: Parking lots in front and rear

Year-round beers: Golden Hawk Wheat, Red Rocket Amber Ale, Bees Knees Honey Ale, Flying Aces Pale Ale, Black Cobra Oatmeal Stout, and Homemade NA Root Beer

Seasonal/limited release beers: About 20 different recipes throughout the year with some regulars thrown in. Irish Red, Hefeweizen, Kolsch, and Oktoberfest return each year as part of the rotation.

Food: American Cuisine

Tip: Travis' Bees Knees Honey Ale uses 25 pounds of local honey in each batch.

Notes:

Toppling Goliath
Brewing
Company
Decorah

BREWING COMPANY
DECORAH, IA

"It all started because I was thirsty for an IPA," says Toppling Goliath Owner Clark Lewey.

The picturesque landscape of Northeast Iowa has a lot to offer, but it has not historically possessed much in the way of hoppy beers. Back in 2009, Clark surveyed the bars and restaurants over a four-county area and couldn't find a single IPA on tap. And so he changed all that.

Though he'd worked in the beverage industry for 30 years and had business-planned a brewery off and on for 10 years, it only took five months of homebrewing for Clark to realize that opening a brewery was actually an urgent matter. He ditched his original plan of opening a brewpub and honed in on a production facility, starting on a half-barrel system. A year and a half later, Clark added a 10-barrel system, and by 2013, TG was brewing on a 30-barrel brewhouse, switched from limited hand-bottled releases to an automated bottling line that would help meet growing demand, and distributing in both Iowa and Wisconsin. But that was no easy task.

Since it opened in 2009, Toppling Goliath in Decorah has earned a reputation for being not just a notable Iowa brewer of hop-forward beers, but also a hop-centric brewery of national acclaim. When word got out about TG's pseudoSue, a Citra-hopped pale ale that some have said could be classified as an IPA, TG became a breakout phenom in beer trader circles and is constantly in short supply in its home state. That's been a double-edged sword. While enthusiasm and demand are good, they make for a lot of work. And while TG has expanded extensively, they still have trouble meeting consumers' expectations. "We can only make so much beer," says Clark, noting that he's got distributors in 15 states hoping to sell his beer well beyond Iowa's borders.

While he likes making pseudoSue, he has other beers he wants to make as well. "I want to make people happy without stopping the creative process," he says. "We do get bored easily." Stop by the taproom, and you're liable to find a brown ale, an Irish red ale, a California common, and a stout—and that's before you get to the hoppy offerings. In addition to their "regular" lineup of pale ales, IPAs and double IPAs, TG has brewed around a dozen (to-date) single-hopped IPA riffs to showcase individual hop varieties in the brewery's Hop Patrol Series.

A number of them feature experimental hops not yet in full production or available on the open market. It's just my luck, but my all-time favorite TG beer was one of these: Riwakan Dead IPA, featuring the low-yield Riwaka hop from New Zealand. Clark's not the only beer drinker that hopes the buzz created by these beers will convince farmers to expand production of some of these hop varieties.

Clark credits Brewmaster Mike Saboe for the lion's share of TG's success. "The world is his hop playground," says Clark. Mike has distinguished himself as one of the premier hop wranglers in the country, but he's no one-trick pony. His imperial stouts Assassin, Mornin' Delight, and Kentucky Brunch have created a stir of their own.

"We prefer extreme brewing," says Clark of the view he shares with Mike. Together, they work to push the edge of what beer can be in Iowa, and gain respect in other parts of the world for their efforts. "When Mike came on board, he gave me the confidence to grow the company," Clark says.

Grow, it has, and if the clamor for and quality of the TG beers to date are any indicator, grow, it will continue to do so.

Get your hop fix at the Toppling Goliath taproom in Decorah.

The Details

Toppling Goliath Brewing Company
310 College Drive (taproom)
1762 Old Stage Road (production brewery)
Decorah, Iowa 52101
(563) 382-6198 (taproom)
(563) 387-6700 (brewery)

Online: tgbbrews.com, Facebook, Twitter
Owners: Clark and Barb Lewey
Brewmaster: Mike Saboe
Year opened: 2009
Brewing systems: ½-barrel, 10-barrel, and 30-barrel
Tours: Call for information
Availability: Bottles and draught in Iowa and Wisconsin
Parking: Yes
Public Transportation: Yes
Year-round beers: Dorothy's New World Lager, Tsunami Pale, and pseudoSue
Seasonal/limited release beers: Assassin, Mornin' Delight, Kentucky Brunch Brand Stout
Annual Events: Assassin Day is an annual release of TG's barrel-aged stouts
Food: No
Local non-beer attractions: Decorah Eagle's Nest, Decorah Trolley Company, Decorah Historic Architecture Tour, Fort Atkinson Preserve, and Laura Ingalls Wilder Museum
Tip: Toppling Goliath has the reputation for being one of the state's best hop-forward brewers, so check these beers out. Everyone seems bananas over pseudoSue, but I loved the apparent one-off, Riwakan Dead IPA. If you ever see it turn up, give it a try!

Notes:

Twisted Vine Brewery

St. Charles

Of all the breweries in Iowa, Twisted Vine Brewery is situated in arguably the most beautiful location of all. Launched in the summer of 2011 by a trio of homebrewing comrades, Brian Sabus, Steve Breman and Steve Becker, Twisted Vine sits among forested rolling hills outside St. Charles, in the land of Madison County's famous covered bridges and only a thirty-minute drive from Des Moines. What's more, this brewery represents one of the greatest business synergies in the state: Twisted Vine built its brewery on space owned by the good folks at Madison County Winery.

Before there was a brewery in this scenic location, there was a winery and a gorgeous tasting room. Madison County Winery owner Doug Baker had chatted with his longtime friend, Brian, about pulling in Brian's commercial brewing aspirations to complement his setup. When Iowa beer laws became favorable to such an enterprise in 2009, Brian and the two Steves made the leap, installing a one-barrel brewing system in a tiny corner of Doug's warehouse.

They were busy from the start. Twisted Vine churns out a wide selection of styles sure to please every drinker: blonde ale, scottish ale, pale ale, porter, and a black IPA. They cover a lot of ground to add dimension to the tasting room's options, and even dabble in barrel aging. The reception to their beers has been so strong that only a year after opening their doors, Twisted Vine purchased a 3.5-barrel brewing system to increase production. This upgrade has made servicing accounts in the Des Moines area easier to handle, while maintaining ample stock on their home turf.

It's fine to drink Twisted Vine beers in other parts of the state, but this is one Iowa brewery that deserves to be visited. The grounds of the vineyard are picturesque even without a beer (or glass of wine) in your hand, but hanging out on the patio in the summertime at twilight with a band playing (and a beer in your hand) is absolutely beautiful. Step inside, and you'll see Doug's background in design. It's clean and classy and a great place to share a drink with a friend—or to meet a new one.

Like many brewers, the Twisted Vine crew has an affinity for hops, and harvest time is a good time to delve deeper into Iowa's contribution to the beer industry, as Twisted Vine hosts a Fresh Hops Festival in October, and makes use of hops from Arrowhead Hops, a hop farm in Madrid, Iowa.

Need a snack? While they don't have a full kitchen, there are chocolate and cheese trays to explore.

Though Twisted Vine is a part-time, nano affair by design, its owners are aware of their success, have expansion plans which include both packaging and a second location, and an understanding that they'll have to devote more and more time to the operation in order to keep up...so keep your eyes peeled for a bright, but twisted, future for this little nugget.

The Details

Twisted Vine Brewery is located at Madison County Winery in rural St Charles.

Twisted Vine Brewery
3021 St. Charles Rd.
St. Charles, Iowa 50240

Online: twistedvinebrewery.com, Facebook
Owners/Brewers: Steve Becker, Steve Breman, and Brian Sabus
Year opened: 2011
Brewing system: 3.5-barrel
Tours: Yes
Availability: On draught in the Des Moines Metro area
Parking: Lot
Public Transportation: NA
Awards received: Black IPA won the 2013 Bitter 16 Challenge at Captain's Quarters in Adel
Year-round beers: Twisted Blonde, RathSkelton the Red, Pirate's Kettle Pale Ale, Black Knight IPA, Whistling Ogre Wheat, Tsunami Porter, Old Crusty's Scottish Ale
Seasonal/limited release beers: Varies. Two hyper-local offerings have been LaPetite Saison (brewed with grape juice from the winery) and Honey Harvest Ale (local Iowa honey from the valley), not to mention the use of Templeton Rye barrels in the brewery's modest barrel program.
Annual events: Fresh Hops Festival in October
Food: Chocolate and cheese platters
Local non-beer attractions: Madison County Winery (onsite), John Wayne Birthplace and the famous Bridges of Madison County
Tip: Twisted Vine Brewery and Madison County Winery play host to live music on the patio in the summer months—a great setting for drinks, music and friends.

Notes:

Van Houzen Brewing Company

Newton

Hiatus. That's the status of Van Houzen Brewing Company, which first started producing beer in 2011.

Owner/Brewer Aren Houzen set up shop in the lower level of the Sugar Grove Gathering Place in Newton, putting out a quartet of high-gravity beers: The Professor, a double IPA; Sacrifish, an American-hopped Belgian tripel; Symphony, an imperial double chocolate stout; and Three-Toed Dog, a unique beer brewed with three grains, a three-step mashing process, and a three-tiered hop schedule.

Though Aren attracted a following among beer lovers at beer festivals and a handful of draught accounts in central and eastern Iowa, the harsh winter of 2013-14 caused plumbing problems, and he was forced to put his brewhouse in storage and regroup.

I spoke with Aren recently, and his plan was to move his facility to eastern Iowa and re-launch. Due to the many factors involved in the process, he had no firm start date, so we'll all just have to wish him the best and wait and see.

The Details

Van Houzen Brewing Company

Online: vhbrewing.com, Facebook
Owners: Aren, Kurt, and Michael Van Houzen
Brewermaster: Aren Van Houzen
Year opened: 2011
Brewing system: 1-barrel
Availability: Currently suspended production
Year-round beers: The Professor, Sacrifish, Symphony, and Three-Toed Dog.
Seasonal/limited release beers: Stoutskyn Series of barrel-aged stouts
Tip: Follow Van Houzen Brewing Company online to monitor its re-launch progress.

Notes:

West O Beer

West Okoboji

It's a common story: West O Beer Company owners Matt and Michaela Matthiesen were homebrewers, and had considered opening a brewery for a number of years. To gain greater insight into the workings of the industry, Matt attended courses at Chicago's Siebel Institute. It was a wise move, which has resulted in uncommon beer.

The original plan was to open a brewpub in Spencer, where the Matthiesens reside, but they realized that this is essentially starting two businesses, a brewery as well as a restaurant, and opted to focus on the beer. They shifted to the packaging brewery concept. A few miles to the north, West Okoboji possessed affordable industrial space; reasonable proximity to larger markets like Sioux Falls, Minneapolis, Omaha, and Des Moines; the lakes for tourist-driven taproom traffic; and great brewing water. And so West O was born.

When the doors opened in 2013, West O owned three 15-barrel fermenters, but once they fired up the bottling line that fall, it became clear that the brewery would require more tank space to meet demand. The Matthiesens purchased three additional 30-barrel fermenters to effectively triple capacity. The drive for West O's demand rests on the shoulders of Brewmaster Karl Schmitz.

Taking a job on Cold Spring Brewery's packaging line in his Minnesota hometown at the age of 18, Karl brewed his first beer a month after he turned 21. In a "now or never" moment of risk, Karl applied for the West O brewmaster's position, a 26-year-old with quite a bit of experience. He liked Matt and Michaela and decided it was a good opportunity for him. "We wanted the same thing out of our beers and the same direction for the company, so it was a good fit," he says. "You never really can be sure about anything, but it was 'if not now, then when?'"

After nine years at Cold Spring, Karl was given "more or less" free reign to build a new family of beers at West O. "The Smoked Red is something that I'd had in my head for a while," he says. "I don't much like smoked beers, but a smoked red ale that has a light amount of smoke in it—I thought would be delicious." Customers agree. The Smoked Red immediately became the brewery's top seller, followed by Schmitz's go-to beer, the Pilsner. "The popularity of [the Smoked Red] speaks for itself," says Karl. "I never thought it was going to be the most popular beer."

While the Smoked Red was a surprise hit, the Pilsner was a beer Karl, a brewer with an affinity for lagers, knew would work well at West O. "Our water is pulled by the city from the West Lake. It affords us a little softer water than if it were coming from a well," he says, commenting on the crucial ingredient.

On the other hand, Karl was never happy with the pale ale he designed for the brewery's original lineup, and on my visit, he explained that he was scrapping it in favor of Holy L, a 4.5% ABV Session IPL (India Pale Lager), an emerging style, and not the last we'll see of Karl's affection for lagers. He hopes to bring his Oktoberfest to market in the fall—his first seasonal release to make it into bottles.

The West O taproom is a good place to try it. With cement flooring and a lot of metal, the space has an industrial feel that emerges from the brewery itself, visible through windows to the left of the bar. West O's tap handles are laser-cut metal and the entire lineup pours through a series of kegs, mounted horizontally behind the bar. It looks very cool.

It's a bonus for the Matthiesens that they possess a little extra land on their lot. After a boisterous welcome from consumers, the need to expand may be a problem they have to confront. For now, they have adequate space, but in time, they may need to expand their walls to meet demand.

West O Beer's Pilsner keeps taproom traffic satisfied after a day's recreation on Lake Okoboji.

The Details
West O Beer
503 Terrace Park Blvd.
West Okoboji, Iowa 51351
(712) 332-8090

Online: westobeer.com, Facebook, Twitter
Owners: Matthew and Michaela Matthiesen
Brewmaster: Karl Schmitz
Year opened: 2013
Brewing system: 15-barrel
Tours: Yes
Availability: Bottles and draught
Parking: Parking lot
Public Transportation: Taxi
Year-round beers: Pilsner, Smoked Red Ale, Session India Pale Lager,
    10Foot10 (DIPA)
Seasonal/limited release beers: Das O Hefeweizen, Westoberfest Lager, Belgian
    Double Pumpkin Spice
Annual events: WestOberfest (last weekend in September), Winter Games
    Celebration (last weekend in January), St. Paddy's Day Celebration
Food: Carry-in or deliveries are welcome.
Local non-beer attractions: Iowa Great Lakes
Did you know?: West O's Pilsner and Smoked Red were the brewery's first bottled
    options to hit the beer aisle.

Notes:

Worth Brewing Company

Northwood

Worth Brewing Company proves that less is sometimes more.

Owner/brewmaster Peter Ausenhus only has a 10-gallon brewing system, but he knows what to do with it. After cutting his brewing teeth at Summit Brewing Company in St. Paul, Minnesota, Peter and his wife, Margaret Bishop, opened Worth Brewing Company in tiny Northwood, Central Avenue Historic District on St. Patrick's Day of 2007. Since that time, Peter has put out small batch after small batch of tasty beer, just the way it was done in the good old days.

Peter and Margaret set out to replicate an earlier time in American history, when many towns (and not just the big ones) had a brewery to call their own. And so Worth Brewing Company, six miles east of I-35 and just south of the Iowa-Minnesota line, brews distinctive beers in a decidedly low volume to service local punters as well as travelers passing through. And so, a word of advice: Worth Brewing offers a really good reason to pass through Northwood.

Why? Let's start with the building. Built in 1886 to house Worth County State Bank, the structure later served as the home of Butler Land Company, before the building would be dominated by utilities companies from 1921 to 2006. Northwood-Kensett Electric Company completed a major "modernization" of the building in 1935, doubling its length and significantly re-tooling the building's façade. People's Gas and Electric, and later Interstate Power Company, then Alliant Energy, in addition to second floor lawyers, utilized the space until Peter and Margaret took over in November of 2006. They pushed the building's look back to its 1935 state, pulling down false ceilings, interior walls and restoring the 1935 cork floors. In addition to making superb, hand-crafted beers, Peter has stained glass talent, and so he integrated his other artistic touch into the renewed Worth Brewing façade.

Inside, the taproom showpiece is the bar, thought to be the original bank teller cage, which has lived in many places since it departed the building in 1906-7. It came to WBC when the Worth County Historical Society received it as a donation, but had no room to display it. Wrapped in an inviting pub atmosphere, it's a beautiful piece of history and a good place to order a beer.

And then there's the brewhouse, a 10-gallon Sabco system, on which Peter brews multiple times a week to slake patrons' thirst with beers like Dillon Clock Stopper, Field Trip IPA, Brown Ale, Sunderland English Mild and Oatmeal Stout. While I like all of his beers, I can't help but appreciate that Peter keeps a "sessionable" beer like

Sunderland on tap. Only 3.5% ABV, but packed with flavor, Sunderland is essentially a "small brown ale" and is great for drinking in quantity while immersed in good conversation among friends. Which is one of the reasons that this tiny brewery in this historic building in the northernmost reaches of Iowa is a must-visit.

The Details

Worth Brewing Company
826 Central Avenue
Northwood, Iowa 50459
(641) 324-9899

Online: worthbrewing.com, Facebook
Owners: Peter Ausenhus and Margaret Bishop
Brewmaster: Peter Ausenhus
Year opened: 2007
Brewing system: 10-gallon
Tours: Yes
Availability: Tap Room only
Parking: Street
Year-round beers: Dillon Clock Stopper, Field Trip IPA, Brown Ale, Sunderland English Mild, and Oatmeal Stout
Annual Events: Oktoberfest (last Saturday in September at the Worth County Fair grounds) and Spring Bock Fest (third Saturday in April at the brewery)

Peter Ausenhus of Worth Brewing Company in Northwood takes a taste of one of their beers during one of Iowa's beer festivals.

Seasonal/limited release beers: New one each month
Food: No, but local restaurants deliver to the taproom.
Local non-beer attractions: Brewery is located in the Northwood Central Avenue Historic District, a nationally registered district. Pick up a free walking tour and guidebook at the brewery.
Tip: Sunderland English Mild is a great, low-alcohol choice if you want to sit back and have a few beers over a conversation.

Notes:

The Essentials: Iowa Beer Itineraries

You just flew into Des Moines, and you have a limited number of days to explore Iowa suds. Here are my recommendations, which may require focus to accomplish. Be sure you have a designated driver.

One Day

Day 1: Leave the airport, and drive straight to Confluence Brewing Company (see page 27), only a few minutes away. For lunch, stop by Exile Brewing Company (see page 40). Zip out to Clive to visit 515 Brewing Company (see page 1). Finish the day with short stops at The Royal Mile and The Red Monk before closing it out at el Bait Shop.

Winter alternative: Skip 515 and Exile, opting instead for Raccoon River Brewing Company (see page 95) and Court Avenue Restaurant and Brewery (see page 30) Both offer good lunch options and are accessible from the Skywalk.

Another option: If you want breweries instead of bars (though el Bait Shop is an absolute must-do so you can sample a wide swath of Iowa-brewed beers all in one location), nix The Royal Mile and The Red Monk and visit Firetrucker Brewing Company (see page 42) in Ankeny or take a trip to Knoxville's Peace Tree Brewing Company (see page 92), just a 45-minute drive away from Des Moines.

Three Days

To the One Day Itinerary, add the following:

Day 2: Do you like hops? End your day in Decorah at Toppling Goliath Brewing Company (see page 110). On your way, you can visit Lake Time Brewery (see page 66) and Mason City Brewing Company (see page 76). If you're really ambitious and have the time, consider Worth Brewing Company (see page 119) as well.

Day 3: Drop south from Decorah to the Cedar Rapids-Iowa City area, where you can tick Lion Bridge Brewing Company (see page 68) Big Grove Brewery (see page 14), and Backpocket Brewery (see page 10) off your to-do list. If you haven't already visited Peace Tree, do this on your way back to Des Moines.

Five Days

A five-day trip allows you to add the following to the forays already planned:

On Day 3, swing past Franklin Street Brewing Company (see page 44), and maybe even Guerrilla Brewing Company (see page 55) and/or SingleSpeed Brewing Company (see page 110) on your way to Cedar Rapids. Take some to loiter in the Cedar

Rapids/Iowa City area, and take the time to check out Millstream Brewing Company (see page 79) in the Amana Colonies, as well as Kalona Brewing Company (see page 61). If the calendar lines up for you to visit Sutliff Cider Company (see page 104) during their weekend hours, do so.

I know it's an isolated-looking trip, but I think you should take a day to visit West O Beer (see page 116). The drive is beautiful, and the downtime will do you some good. You can visit Boone Valley Brewing Company (see page 17) on your way, and can check out Okoboji Brewing Company (see page 86) while you're in the neighborhood. That, and you can enjoy the outdoor recreation offered by Lake Okoboji.

Seven Days

Seven days gives you the freedom to add Great River Brewery (see page 52)to the plan and linger at all your stops. Also, work Boone Valley into a self-identified (see page 52) lull in your schedule and make that Okoboji Day a Western Iowa Day, making stops at Keg Creek Brewing Company (see page 63) CIB Brewery (see page 25) once their taproom opens, and Brick Street Brewing Company (see page 20). Consider a stop at Twisted Vine Brewery (see page 113).

If you can time it to be in the Waterloo area on a Thursday, you need to try to catch a beer release at Guerrilla Brewing Company (see page 55). While you're close by, check out SingleSpeed Brewing Company (see page 102) in Cedar Falls.

Passing Through

Let's say you're passing through Iowa on I-80 or I-35. In that case, here's my advice for the person who's not in the driver's seat:

I-80 (west to east)

An immediate side trip is required once you enter the state from Nebraska: either go north toward Brick Street Brewing Company (see page 20), south to Keg Creek Brewing Company (see page 63), or head east for a short distance before veering south to CIB Brewery (see page 25). Next up: Des Moines, which offers options. Try Exile Brewing Company (see page 40), Raccoon River Brewing Company (see page 95), or Confluence Brewing Company (see page 27). Also, stop by el Bait Shop for the best chance to taste Iowa-brewed beers that aren't available along the interstate. If you want to grab a beer and a funky bite to eat, check out Zombie Burger in the East Village. A little further to the east, you'll run across Millstream Brewing Company (see page 79) in the Amana Colonies and Backpocket Brewing Company (see page 10), a must-stop. Then finish out with Great River Brewery (see page 52) in Davenport.

I-35 (south to north)

If you have time for an hour-trek to the east, Albia Brewing Company (see page 3) has both good beer and a beautiful building to check out. If not, keep going north to pay a visit to Twisted Vine Brewery (see page 113). For this Des Moines pass-through, hit Rock Bottom Restaurant and Brewery (see page 97) and/or 515 Brewing Company (see page 1). Swing by Firetrucker Brewing Company (see page 42) before making your final northward push to Worth Brewing Company (see page 119), just east of the interstate and a little shy of the Minnesota border.

Notable Beers

No matter the makeup of your trip, here are a few beers you should try if you get the chance.

Backpocket Brewing Company's Slingshot Dunkel (smooth and dark) or Wooden Nickel (a unique German-Scottish hybrid)

New American Brewing Company's 1789 Porter (solid for dark beer lovers)

Millstream Brewing Company's Schild Brau Amber Lager (an award-winning Iowa classic) or John's Generations White Ale

Great River Brewery's Redband Coffee Stout (you can't drink all day if you don't start with a coffee beer in the morning)

Rock Bottom Restaurant and Brewery's barrel-aged beers or Wild Things series

Keg Creek Brewing Company's Black Lager (a good growler fill if you can swing it)

CIB Brewery's Dethhanger Quadruple Brown Ale (big, complex and packed with *terroir*)

West O Beer's Pilsner and Smoked Red (because they're delicious)

Exile Brewing Company's Ruthie (an easy-drinking Munich helles)

Boone Valley Brewing Company's Barrel-aged Imperial Roxie (if this big, red ale ever returns)

Toppling Goliath Brewing Company's pseudoSue Pale Ale (TG's earned a lot of notoriety around the country with this one, among others)

Sutliff Cider is light and refreshing

Peace Tree Brewing Company's Red Rambler if you're grilling or the Hop Wrangler for a Belgian twist on an IPA

Confluence Brewing Company's Des Moines IPA or Oktoberfest, depending on your mood

Still Fermenting

In addition to the 56 breweries profiled in Iowa Pints, there are, to date, roughly 28 breweries-in-planning that Iowa beer drinkers have to look forward to. A difficult list to track, here are just a few upstarts ranging from pipe dream to sure thing which Iowa imbibers can expect to add to the beery landscape in the future.

Adel
Panfish Brewing Company

Ames
Alluvial Brewing Company
Torrent Brewing Company
Ames Brewery-in-Planning

Cedar Rapids
Iowa Brewing Company
Palindrome Brewing Company
Quarter Barrel
Slew City Brewing Company
Turner Alley Brewing Company

Clive
Brewery-in-Planning

Des Moines
Black Hollow Brewing Company
Flix Brewhouse
Heartbreak Brewery
Hopheads Brewing Company
Kyte Brewing Company

Dubuque
Catfish Charlie's
Dubuque Star Brands

Iowa City
Brewery-in-Planning

Jefferson Township
Brewery-in-Planning

Lake Charles
Brewery-in-Planning

La Porte City
P n B's Brew Pub

Manson
Bulldawg Brew

Polk City
Liberty's Forge Brewing Company

Shelby
Willow Creek Glass Chapel

Sioux City
Sioux City Suds
Hard Rock Hotel
Brewery-in-Planning

Undetermined Location
Liberty's Forge Brewing Company

Andy McCormick of Madrid's Arrowhead Hop Farm will open Torrent Brewing Company in Ames.

Better Beer Bars & Restaurants

Compiled with the help of Iowa beer lovers, brewers, and distributors, here are 55 pro-drinker recommended places to find a good beer in Iowa.

Adel
Captain's Quarters

Algona
Billie Jo's Bar & Grill

Ames
DG's Tap House
Dublin Bay
Es Tas
London Underground
Mucky Duck
Old Chicago

Ankeny
Old Chicago

Bettendorf
Old Chicago

Burlington
Moto's Public House

Carson
Back 40

Cedar Falls
Mulligan's Brick Oven Grill & Pub
Old Chicago

Cedar Rapids
Parlor City Pub & Eatery

Coralville
Old Chicago

Council Bluffs
1892

Davenport
Sippy's

Des Moines
The Cheese Shop
el Bait Shop
The Exchange
Fong's Pizza
Hessen Haus
Old Chicago
Red Monk
The Riverwalk Hub
Royal Mile
University Library Café
Up-Down
Wellman's Pub
Zombie Burger

Dubuque
Eronel
The Lift
Monk's Kaffee Pub

Elkader
Schera's

Fort Madison
Horan's Cabaret

Iowa City
Clinton Street Social Club
The Sanctuary
Short's Burgers & Shine
Stella's

La Porte City
P n B's Brew Pub

Le Claire
Biere Stube

Marion
Ramsey's Metro Market

North Liberty
Reds Alehouse

Orange City
Blue Mountain Culinary Emporium

Oskaloosa
Cellar Peanut Pub

Oxford
Augusta

Sioux City
4th Street Sports Grill
Soho Kitchen & Bar
The House of Q

Stone City
Stone City General Store

Waterloo
The Beer Hall
Lava Lounge

West Des Moines
The Keg Stand
Wellman's Pub

Better Beer Aisles*

Headed to a party or barbecue and need to take something along? Here are a few of Iowa's best beer aisles.

Ames
Wheatsfield Cooperative

Cedar Rapids
Benz Beverage Depot
NewBo City Market

Des Moines
Gateway Market

Iowa City
John's Grocery

Sioux City
Charlie's Wine and Spirits

Urbandale
Beer Crazy

West Des Moines
Whole Foods Market

*Hy-Vee has dozens of beer-friendly locations all across the state

Iowa Homebrew Clubs

Looking to bond with fellow Iowa zymurgists? Many homebrew (and just beer appreciation) clubs meet throughout the state to taste, discuss and brew better beers together.

Ames
Ames Brewers League

Burlington
Burlingon MOB (Makers of Beer)

Cedar Falls/Waterloo
Cedar River Association of Zymurgy Enthusiasts

Cedar Rapids
Cedar Rapids Beer Nuts

Cherokee
Cherokee Brewers

Clear Lake
North Iowa Wine Club

Corning
Adams County Brew Crew (AC/BC)

Davenport
MUGZ
River's Edge Fermentation Society

Denver
Brewers of Bremer County (BoBCo)

Des Moines
Barley's Angels
Iowa Brewers Union (IBU)
Powder Keggers
Raccoon River Brewers Association

Dubuque
GotMead International Brewmasters
Dubuque Area Society of Brewers (DaSOB)

Elkader
Turkey River Utopian Brewers (TRUBs)

Fort Madison
Makers of Beer (MOB)

Glenwood
Keg Creek Homebrewers

Iowa City
THIRSTY

Milford
Okoboji Hombrewers Guild

Monroe
Cenosilicaphobia Club

Northwood
Iowa/Minnesota Society of Brewers (IAMNSOB)

Oskaloosa
Oskaloosa Beer Brewers

Schleswig
Schleswig Wine & Bier Club

Sioux City
RASCALS

Iowa Homebrew Shops

Tasted something inspiring and want to try your hand at brewing beer at home?
Try one of these homebrew shops to pave your way to your own lineup of beers.

Ankeny
C&S Brew Supply

Atlantic
Harvest Moon Market

Decorah
From Grain to Glass

Des Moines
Heartland Homebrew Supply

Dubuque
Bluff Street Brew Haus

Elkader
Deb's Brewtopia

Marion
BIY Homebrew Supply

Ottumwa
Central Homebrew Supply

Parkersburg
BlueStem Winery

Cedar Falls
Kitchen Wines and Brew Shop

Spirit Lake
Okoboji Brewing Company

Urbandale
Beer Crazy

Iowa Pints Extras

(Left) First come first served at Brick Street Brewing Company, but there is alway time for a little shop talk with a customer.

(Right) The Little Giant Beer Summit is one of many beer festivals showcasing the beers brewed in Iowa.

(Above) Lunch goers enjoy conversation at Appanoose Rapids Brewing Company in Ottumwa.

(Above) Exile Brewing Company in Des Moines focuses on brewing German-influenced lagers.

(Right) Constantly rotating its offerings keeps beer drinkers on their toes at SingleSpeed Brewing Company in Cedar Falls.

(Above) Rustic Brewing in Hampton offers boths kinds of brew beer and coffee in a quaint atmosphere.

(Right)Freshly canned Great River Brewing's 483 Pale Ale makes its way toward grocery stores aisles for thirty consumers

(Right) Brewing big beer on a small system, Worth Brewing Company was one of Iowa's original namo-breweries.

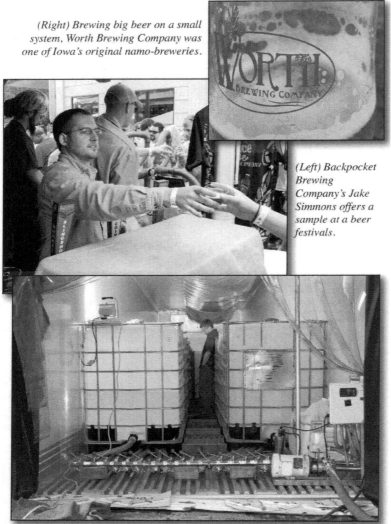

(Left) Backpocket Brewing Company's Jake Simmons offers a sample at a beer festivals.

(Above) A worker transfers unfermented wort to a truck for shipping to one of the Granite City Food and Brewery locations, where it will ferment prior to serving.

Acknowledgments

Due to my beery content, I find it necessary to express my gratitude first to my wife, Michelle, and my two boys, Jake and Tom. They put up with a lot of extra beer detours during otherwise family outings, as well as complete disappearances of dear old dad during my preparation for this book. I'm very grateful for their willingness to play along with having a so-called "beer writer" in their family.

This book could not have been possible without the cooperation of Iowa's brewers and brewery owners. They allowed me to invade their space, pick their brains, taste their beers, and shoot photos, and many followed up with ongoing email conversations to help me solidify the content in their entries.

Thanks to those kind souls who helped out with proofreading duties: Marty Olive, Jacki Bardole, and Michelle Wilson.

Thanks to Tim Hynds and Paul Kavulak for their assistance with procuring historical information.

Though not a brewer, Jeff Bruning has been a key player in the development of Iowa's craft beer scene, and I'm grateful that he lent his support by writing the foreword and agreeing to host the book's release party at el Bait Shop.

And finally, I'd like to thank my publishers, Don and Christy Groves, for their hard work and support.

About the Author

J. Wilson is an award-winning homebrewer, BJCP certified beer judge and Minister of Iowa Beer at the Iowa Brewers Guild. Blogging about an ideal condition of harmony, beer and joy at brewvana.net since 2007, Wilson is the author of the 2011 investigation into the origins of doppelbock, *Diary of a Part-Time Monk*. Named Wynkoop Brewing Company's 2012 Beer Drinker of the Year, Wilson lives in rural Adams County, Iowa with his wife and two sons.